Psychotherapy, American Culture, and Social Policy

Culture, Mind, and Society

The Book Series of the Society for Psychological Anthropology

With its book series Culture, Mind, and Society and journal *Ethos*, the Society for Psychological Anthropology publishes innovative research in culture and psychology now emerging from the discipline of anthropology and related fields. As anthropologists seek to bridge gaps between ideation and emotion or agency and structure—and as psychologists, psychiatrists, and medical anthropologists search for ways to engage with cultural meaning and difference—this interdisciplinary terrain is more active than ever.

This book series from the Society for Psychological Anthropology establishes a forum for the publication of books of the highest quality that illuminate the workings of the human mind, in all of its psychological and biological complexity, within the social, cultural, and political contexts that shape thought, emotion, and experience.

Titles in the Series

Adrie Kusserow, *American Individualisms: Child Rearing and Social Class in Three Neighborhoods*

Naomi Quinn, editor, *Finding Culture in Talk: A Collection of Methods*

Anna Mansson McGinty, *Becoming Muslim: Western Women's Conversions to Islam*

Psychotherapy, American Culture, and Social Policy

Immoral Individualism

Elizabeth A. Throop

palgrave
macmillan

PSYCHOTHERAPY, AMERICAN CULTURE, AND SOCIAL POLICY

First published in 2009 by
PALGRAVE MACMILLAN®
in the United States—a division of St. Martin's Press LLC,
175 Fifth Avenue, New York, NY 10010.

Where this book is distributed in the UK, Europe and the rest of the world, this is by Palgrave Macmillan, a division of Macmillan Publishers Limited, registered in England, company number 785998, of Houndmills, Basingstoke, Hampshire RG21 6XS.

Palgrave Macmillan is the global academic imprint of the above companies and has companies and representatives throughout the world.

Palgrave® and Macmillan® are registered trademarks in the United States, the United Kingdom, Europe and other countries.

ISBN-13: 978–0–230–60945–7
ISBN-10: 0–230–60945–7

Library of Congress Cataloging-in-Publication Data is available from the Library of Congress.

A catalogue record of the book is available from the British Library.

Design by Newgen Imaging Systems (P) Ltd., Chennai, India.

First edition: January 2009

10 9 8 7 6 5 4 3 2 1

Printed in the United States of America.

Contents

Introduction

This is a book born of outrage. For decades now I have observed American culture and I remain perplexed at the inability of Americans to understand their behavior as learned, as harmful, and as supremely selfish. Both as a social worker–cum-family therapist and as a cultural anthropologist, I have watched the United States grow more and more insular even as the world imposes itself on us-economically to be sure but violently as well. For decades now I have heard the explanations for America's appalling high rates of violence, for America's dismal performance intellectually, for America's astonishingly high rates of poverty, child murder, and infant mortality rates. Those explanations never rang true for me. Where, I kept wondering, were the rest of us when children murder, or are murdered? Where are the rest of us when men rape their daughters? Where are the rest of us when drugs take hold of poor communities? I kept hearing about personal responsibility. I rarely heard anything sensible about social responsibility.

So I grew more and more disturbed, and more and more outraged, and more and more ashamed of my country. My family has been part of this country since Puritan times; I have a stake in the United States. And so I wrote this book as a way to analyze my own culture, and criticize it as I hope to make it better. It is a truism that anthropologists aim not to change the culture they study—but I always except their home cultures from this rule. We are allowed to comment on, criticize, and try to change our own societies.

I love the United States. I love our optimism, our ability to get things done, our hopes and our dreams, our humor and our skills. I know we can do better than we have and than we are. I wrote this book—a polemic, almost—to shock you, to provoke you, to make you think about your place in this country and our place in this world. I wrote the book to force a confrontation. I know I will get one. I hope, following the confrontation, we can have a conversation.

The ideas and outrage in this book are entirely my own. I do want to acknowledge the intellectual history of this book, however. I have been thinking about these ideas for close to twenty years, but reading Bellah et al.'s *Habits of the Heart*, and coming to know Dick Madsen very well, crystallized a number of ideas for me. Dick and his colleagues have analyzed some of the same things in a different, and, I think, a more grace-filled way, than have I. Nonetheless, Bellah and his colleagues had a profound effect on my intellectual life. So too did Bill Epstein's various works taking apart psychotherapy and social science "research." I owe Bill a significant debt and I am grateful for his intellectual trailblazing and inspiration. Work by Barbara Ehrenreich, Arlie Hoschild, Marc Swartz, Meredith Small, Sarah Blaffer Hrdy, Kutchins and Kirk, Specht and Courtney, Paul Krugman, Mark Rank, Jonathan Marks, and Robert Reich have all influenced me as well.

Discussions with Bob McCaslin, Stephanie Adams, Peter Zelles, various individuals who participate in an online academic forum, Stacy Veeder, Bob Karolich, Gerald Duff and Pat Stephens, Phil Neale, and numerous students over the years have helped me hone and refine my ideas. All mistakes, exaggerations, overstatements, touches of megalomania, misinterpretations, and offensive sentiments are mine, though of course we all bear responsibility for such things.

Chapter 1

American Culture in Cross-cultural Context

The American dominant cultural elevation of the individual self as the sole locus of motivation, perception, thought, emotion, and behavior is reflected in social policy, both as officially enacted and as understood popularly. We see this in policy dealing with family life, sexuality, psychotherapy, juvenile "offenders," mental illness, welfare, and education. In this book, I describe and analyze the peculiarly American set of cultural understandings concerning the construction of self-in-society as it relates to common understandings of state and national governmental policies mediating the relationship between persons and the state. Throughout, I blend my training and experiences both as a psychological anthropologist and as a social worker and family therapist. Individualistic explanations for behavior and so forth may or may not be completely inaccurate. My interest here, though, is in exploring a more complex analysis of what may be involved in problematic behaviors. I am not necessarily arguing that psychotherapy, for instance, or psychopharmacology that focuses on individual functioning (for instance) is entirely ineffective or harmful; but neither activity is enough if the reduction of suffering is one of the aims of a moral (a "good") society. Indeed, objective empirical evidence indicates that few forms of psychotherapy and psychopharmacology ameliorate the larger cultural and systemic issues I am discussing (Epstein 1997: 182–195; Epstein 1995, 2006; Specht and Courtney 1994: 30–50). I take the elimination, or at least the reduction, of suffering as an essential principle of a good and moral society.

Immediately, we must establish that individualism, using historical and anthropological frameworks, is specifically American, or, at the least, that there is a form of exaggerated individualism that is uniquely American. At the same, the general rejection of larger cultural and systemic analyses of actions and motivations must be shown. The unusual nature of this set of cultural understandings can be shown through a preliminary cross-cultural comparison of personhood after some basic precepts of American cultural understandings are established as being both historically rooted and extant today.

The construction of the individual self in American society

The self in America, both historically and currently, stands in opposition to the family, community, and nation. It is also an unusual construction of the individual cross-culturally. Only in the United States does the insistence hold sway that the individual is almost entirely self-made. Attempts by some Americans—largely academics, clerics (such as the National Conference of Catholic Bishops' letter on American economic policies in 1986 [cited in Bellah et al. 1988]), or labor leaders—to demonstrate the connections between self and other have been and continue to be roundly rejected by dominant ideology and culture.

From where did this overweening sense of individualism come? We know that the United States was colonized by politically and religiously disaffected English men and women in the early seventeenth century who wished to live communal, pure, and simple lives. Individualism as we understand it now did not really begin until after the Civil War with the rise of industrialism, though of course there were hints of it right from the start.

Mercantilism, for instance, became established, slowly to be sure, as the colonies' populations grew. Subsistence farming dwindled with more people and particularly more single settlers. A growth in urbanism prior to the American Revolution reflected the fact that fewer families were farming simply for themselves; a shift to cash crop farming marked a growing occupational specialization in America.

That shift had profound effects on family life. Earlier forms of extended family farms, with the contributions of all family members understood as valuable, began disappearing. Men began assuming responsibility for "outside" work, which in itself began to be see as more valuable than women's work around the homeplace (for cross-cultural examples, see Rogers 1975; Yanagisako 1987). In most societies, a result of the separation of work and home includes a heightened intensity for emotional life inside the home. Gender constructions begin to change as well, with women's work and behaviors being devalued and male work and behavior extolled. As is true in many other societies, in colonial America, women began to be seen as responsible for home life, nurturance, and family organization; any other work they might perform was understood as ancillary to their "real" job—care of the family. Men, on the other hand, began to be constructed as rational, strong, and the head of the family. Gender polarization is one of many strands involved in the weaving of American individualism. Full-bore industrialism was another.

Even though the nascent American industrialization actually resulted in a heightened interdependence between various sectors in the economy, that interdependence was not easy to see (Bellah et al. 1985: 44). Instead, as the possibility (though, of course, not the reality) of "getting ahead" through hard work at the factory or the office emerged, individuals increasingly split their lives into smaller and smaller segments. One did one thing—and adopted one persona—at work and looked to the home as the place for intimacy and love, a place to be one's real self. One's position in the community became divorced from the workplace and the home; a clear demarcation between private and public lives became necessary (Throop 1999: 8–19).

In this cultural construction, one that polarized gender behaviors in ways Americans had not quite seen before, one was not to bring emotion into the workplace (believed to be male), and the family (believed to be an emotional haven, as were women) was to provide the antidote for the "rationality" of the office (Throop 1999: 8–19). As Bellah et al. point out, "domesticity, love, and intimacy increasingly became 'havens' against the competitive culture of work" (1985: 43). This meant that one's true "individuality" was thought to only be expressed among family and friends, and this in turn led to the notion that if problems emerge they must be the result of an individual failure to recognize and enact oneself with unfettered authenticity of self through effort and work.

American perfectibility

At the same time, at least in Victorian America, the middle classes—themselves a new formation—focused on the control of emotions in many places, not just work. Historian John Kasson notes that, especially for the urban middle classes, emotional expression and manners assumed an unusual place in American behavior. Today's self-help movements recall etiquette advice of the 1900s; Kasson argues that "[e]motions needed to be harnessed in the service of character, and a principal means to do this was through the rein of habit" (Kasson

1990: 154). While not the first example of individualism, certainly the focus of Victorian American etiquette was exquisite attention to oneself and one's emotion, if only to express it appropriately or not at all. Victorian American manners, as well as other nineteenth century movements, reflected the growing interest in understanding the self and, more specifically, one's feelings (even if the aim of those etiquette writers was rigid self-control).

Another nineteenth century movement also peculiar to the United States were the various sets of communal experiments. America may well be unique in its attempts to create perfect societies, from Amish settlements to present-day Mormons. Embedded within these movements, as in etiquette instruction, is the notion that human nature is perfectible. For utopians, the belief is reflected in a deliberate construction of a small, face-to-face society, most often removed from the larger society, in which conditions would exist for transcendence, communion with God, exquisite pleasure, or other such earthly and spiritual delights. That such a place could even be imagined seems to be a clear reflection of American optimism.

Beginning, perhaps, with Governor Winthrop's famous declaration that America, and Massachusetts more specifically, was a new Jerusalem, that shining city on the hill, a beacon for the world, a notion of American and human perfectibility has permeated American culture. The Declaration of Independence aims to form a "more perfect" union; clearly the possibility was envisioned. Utopias provide another example, as do the various moral movements, particularly of the nineteenth century (such as temperance, muscular Christianity, the Great Revival, anti-evolutionism, and scientific management, among many others). The Progressive Era, in which social reforms sincerely were thought to be right, moral, necessary, and effective, reflects this optimism yet again (Gordon 1992, 1994). It is only with the Great Depression that we see just a bit of a faltering in American optimism, but the designers of the New Deal seemed to believe that the programs envisioned and enacted would solve America's problems, especially backed by "science," as was claimed (Gordon 1992).

America's belief in science, and progress, and perfectibility, continues today. The legacy of World War II, the cold war, Vietnam, the Gulf War, and, most recently, radical Muslim terrorism, could have mounted serious challenges to America's perennial optimism. Instead, each conflict provided Americans with a choice—understand the country in a larger global context, or understand one's personal reactions to the conflicts. Overwhelmingly, Americans have chosen to understand themselves in relation only to themselves. And our culture has encouraged such beliefs. Our notion that we can improve ourselves, without much help from anyone else, is firmly embedded in our history. All we really need to do is work on ourselves.

Individualism today

And note that last word: work became the icon around which all life revolves. If a person was poor, it became clear that she was poor due to some sort of individual deficiency, an inability to work. If a person had bad relationships, it was because he wasn't working on himself or his relationships enough. Echoing the Calvinist traditions that in part founded this society and that have shaped the culture, individuals and their apparent ability and willingness to work determine their fortunes. Anything else is read as a refusal to take responsibility.

This continues today. Eventually influenced by Freud's brilliant and revolutionary explorations and constructions of the self, Americans are convinced that, contrary to John Donne, every man (and woman) is an island. Freud created a paradigm of individual motivation that persists. We may disagree with his assertions of the primacy of the instincts as motivation for behavior, but we have not rejected on Freud's belief that an individual, in American interpretations, is, as anthropologist Clifford Geertz (1975: 48) put it, "a bounded, unique, more or less integrated motivational and cognitive universe, a dynamic center of awareness, emotion, judgment, and action organized into a distinctive whole and set contrastively against other such wholes and against a social and natural background...." Americans believe that we behave because we choose to; or, if we do not precisely choose to, it is because we are confused or ill. We do not accept an alternate hypothesis, that we might behave because the culture and the systems in which we interact shape our behaviors, motivations, thoughts, beliefs, or feelings. We do not believe we are culturally constructed. Instead, uncritically, we believe we act as nature tells us to act. And we believe all humans are similarly motivated—we see dominant American cultural beliefs, erroneously, as universal and thus natural, biologically based, a very ethnocentric view.

Mainly, we explain ourselves and our behaviors by alluding to emotions—thought to be individually motivated, experienced, and expressed—that give rise to behaviors. Americans tend to "psychologize" behavior. That is, we tend to explain behavior as coming from an individualized, internal mechanism that we call "the mind" or "the self" or "the personality" over which we often have some control. This stands in opposition to most societies of the world, which see troubles as arising from unhappy ancestor spirits, magic, or angry gods, due to kinship or other social offenses (see further on). But in the dominant culture of the United States, there is a fair amount of discussion these days about what is called "personal responsibility," invoking individualistic explanations for behaviors.

Indeed, Americans do not support other kinds of explanations. Our nostalgic view of our history, our support for rugged individualism, can be seen in our demands for individual responsibility for actions, outcomes, and feelings. We see it as well in our belief that persons should be—indeed, have a drive to be—autonomous and independent. It is reflected in our beliefs that our emotions are knowable and controllable and understandable—and interesting. Even within the family today, we believe that each child is unique, special, and interesting; we believe that each family member has thoughts, emotions, and beliefs that should be explored, discussed, and shared. Our definition of family, of course, is rather an impoverished one. We tend to believe that the "nuclear" family is natural, traditional, and healthy (it is none of those things, of course; see chapter 4); this too reflects our belief in individualism as we have rejected extended family organizations for a much smaller constellation—one that is very, perhaps pathologically, emotionally intense.

The bounded self

Anthropologists typically draw the distinction between notions of the Western autonomous self and the non-Western contextualized self by examining an individual's explanations for her own or others' behaviors. If the individual accounts for her behavior with reference to her own motivations, desires, abilities, or characteristics, she displays a "bounded self." She does what she does because she wants to or is intrapsychically driven to do so; she interacts with others based on her perception of herself as a discrete being, impermeable and responsible for her own actions. She can know herself apart from others, and she acts apart from others, making her own decisions without reference to anyone but herself.

Clifford Geertz describes the Western conceptualization of self as a concrete, separate, non-contextualized entity. He asserts that the Western notion of self is that "bounded universe" noted earlier.

The Western concept of the person as autonomous and separate is not universal as had been assumed. Instead, it is European and probably more specifically American.

The bounded self arose partly in conjunction with the Protestant Reformation and the Enlightenment. Gaines (1982) argues that these movements provided northern Europeans in particular with a new concept of the individual as captain of his soul (183). Gaines contends that this new individualism, which he terms a "referential" self, came to be seen as changeable but complete; as the European intellectual ideology, particularly that of science, developed, the self came to be seen as able to renew himself, alter himself, with a strong enough will (182).

This view of the self as a work in process expanded and medicine and psychoanalysis—and other forms of psychotherapy—were formulated (indeed, it was a necessary precondition for psychotherapy). Today, says Gaines, at least within the context of psychotherapy, the individual sees herself and is seen by therapists

> as capable of instituting personal change, almost at will. One is capable of making himself or herself over, and may be expected to do so if problems in relationships or occupation develop. Change is viewed as positive, both as it relates to the individual and to other elements in the behavioral environment...The person is seen, implicitly, as an empirical, real entity. (Gaines 1982: 182–183)

The individual is a discrete, bounded entity who has or should have control over her actions, emotions, and life in the Western conceptualization of self.

The Western idea of self as autonomous and controlled (or controllable) figures heavily in psychological and ethnographic research. White and Marsella (1982) contend that Western models of the self facilitate a "psychologization" of behavior on the part of both researchers and the public:

> In so far as the self is more readily abstracted from social contexts and becomes an object of reflection, it is not surprising that the notion of "psychology" itself looms so large in both popular and professional views of social experience in Western society; that a great deal of concern focuses on personal "identity" or the "ego" as an integrated and continuous expression of the person; and that various forms of illness and mental disorder are characterized as disruptions in the

> unity of continuity of ego integration. (White and Marsella 1982: 21–22)

White and Marsella see the uniquely Western experience of the integrated, reflective, bounded self as erroneously informing research programs, which are based on false assumptions that this conceptualization is universal. They would hesitate at accepting explanations for non-Western behavior that are rooted in these assumptions; perhaps it is as erroneous to use this model as informative for Western behavior as well. At the least, however, it appears that the Western idea of self is not appropriately applied cross-culturally.

Ethnographers studying "mental illness" in non-Western cultures may wrongly apply Western notions of the bounded self in their research. Fabrega (1982) contends that the idea of mental illness is a strictly Western one (he may not be correct there; see Murphy 1976). He identifies several factors in European history that have led to the concept of mental illness:

> 1) the development of the idea of an inner entity or force "behind" human action, termed mind, psyche, etc. as opposed to the body; 2) the emphasis of the Greeks (especially Plato) on the rational and irrational, and the equating of the latter with "disease"; 3) the Hippocratic emphasis on natural causes of disease, and, in general, the heavy somatic emphasis of Graeco-Roman medicine (i.e., that so-called mental illnesses or symptoms were caused by physical disorders)...(Fabrega 1982: 44)

The bounded self, based on "the seemingly obvious notion that a person acts on the basis of a bundle of feelings, motives, and intentions, housed within the individual" (White 1982: 87) is seen by Western researchers and laymen alike to develop mental illness separate from what we see as bodily illnesses.

Explanations for genetic causes of, for instance, anorexia (a quintessentially American "mental illness") include a medical cure, to be sure (or, at least, the is the hoped-for end of current research). However, anorexia remains, in the Western psychiatric community, located in the "mind" separate from the body, and it is housed within an individual's mind—not a social mind—as well. It remains an individual, not physical, illness. The bounded self contains all the elements necessary to develop anorexia: intrapsychic processes, genetic abnormalities (or so it is claimed), inadequate or skewed neural processing. Mental illness, like the self, is based in the individual, and in the individual's mind, divorced from the body.

We can see, then, that the Western conceptualization and experience of self is exclusively individual. Westerners believe that the self is a separate, discrete, autonomous, willful being, able to control her life, her body, her emotions, and her mind, all of which are seen as bounded parts of a bounded self. If problems in societal functioning develop, the individual is the locus of treatment. The individual can change herself (with therapeutic help) in isolation from others; in fact, she is encouraged not to blame anyone but herself for her difficulties.

Received psychological and psychiatric wisdom holds that there are universal psychological processes that rule an individual's emotional life, based on her own configurations of key events and developmental factors in her past (see chapter two for further discussion). These processes are intrapsychic and idiosyncratic within a larger universal framework. That is, while everyone is understood as a unique individual, at least in psychological "personality" theory, it is claimed that there are generally predictable patterns of behavior and stages of development that all humans experience (though such statements are made with almost no cross-cultural evidence; it may be more accurate to say that these are middle-class Western European and American behaviors and stages, though even that has not been proven scientifically as has been claimed). So the Western self is seen as inviolate and nonpermeable—as it should be, according to the "experts"—even with the various tasks the psychiatric and psychological communities says it must perform to become normal. The problem, of course, is that this formulation of identity has little to do with universal psychological functioning.

The diffuse self

In the anthropological literature anyway, the bounded self is often presented in contrast to some other notion of self, typically Asian but sometimes southern European as opposed to northern European (e.g., Gaines 1982). I term this other notion the "diffuse self." The diffuse self is marked in many ethnographies of non-Western cultures by loose boundaries between self and other, allocation of responsibility for difficulties to agencies outside the self as well as within the self, somatic explanations for emotional conflicts (though interestingly Western commentators do not mark emotional difficulties as cover-ups for somatic dysfunctions), contextual situations eliciting different behaviors at different times, and concrete thinking as opposed to the high level of abstraction claimed to be connected with the bounded self.

Scholars of Japanese culture, for instance, note the Japanese self, particularly the female Japanese self, as diffuse. That is, the Japanese self is marked by a lack of boundaries between a discrete self and a discrete other (Lebra 1982; Lock 1982). According to these anthropologists, Japanese persons do not feel a strong sense of self separate from others. Instead, as Lebra remarks

> there is no clear-cut demarcation line between self and other. The identity of self is actually interchangeable with that of another. Identity interchange is acceptable and morally plausible in Japanese culture insofar as identity is framed within the concept of social role. (Lebra 1982: 275)

That is, the Japanese self (as well as other Asian variations), variously called allocentric, sociocentric, or what I am calling a diffuse self, stands as situationally constructed rather than independently existing outside of social context.

Indeed, the anthropological literature on India illustrates the diffuse self quite well. Shweder and Bourne (1991) name the sense of Indian identity the "holistic" self. They argue that the Indian holistic self does not abstract personality characteristics but instead places behavior and events within specific contexts:

> The holistic model, the sociocentric premise, and the organic metaphor focus one's attention on the context-dependent relationship of part to part and part to whole; the holist, convinced that objects and events are necessarily altered by the relations into which they enter, is theoretically primed to contextualize objects and events, and theoretically disinclined to appraise things *in vacuo*, in the abstract. (Shweder and Bourne 1991: 153)

Indians see themselves and others as enmeshed, tied together in relationships, situated in specific contexts and behaviors, unlike the abstract, free-standing, bounded self of the West. Roland calls this the "we-self" (as opposed to the Western "I-self") (1988: 224–225). He notes that Indians have a constant sense of "we-ness," rather than understandings themselves as completely separate, emotionally and behaviorally, from one another. They think of themselves in relation to others in the hierarchical scheme of things. Generally, it is relationships and permeability of relationships and self that are valued by Hindus (there is an inner, private self, unrevealed to anyone, unlike many Americans, who will talk about themselves at the drop of a hat).

Indians, and other Asians, and indeed all humans, learn the cultural models for a sense of identity from birth (or perhaps even before). A discussion of child-rearing practices and ideologies will help illustrate the techniques humans use to teach each other how to understand oneself.

Child-rearing in India

India will illustrate the point nicely. Roland (1988) and Kurtz (1992) argue separately that Indian child-rearing takes place in a context of rural extended family life. Since 70% of the Indian population lives in rural areas, this model can be taken as typical for most Indians. In addition, despite some minor variations, cultural traditions of at least two millennia seem to trump religious beliefs. That is, it does not seem to matter if one is Hindu, Muslim, Sikh, Christian, or Jewish; child-rearing practices are remarkably similar regardless of religion. The key to understanding Indian identity appears to be each person's placement in an extended family unit.

Roland (1988) argues that Indian life, including family life, is intensely and comfortably hierarchical. Indians understand themselves as placed in a number of different structural arrangements. Sometimes they are superior in a set of relationships; sometimes they are subordinate. A particular Indian's behavior depends on the particular situation in which she is placed at any given time. Consistency of behavior, thought, emotion, or belief is not expected. Indians understand that context is all.

Along with context, a deep and abiding belief in karma and reincarnation permeates Indian child-rearing. The concept of karma—destiny or fate as decided by the supernatural—translates, in Indian child-rearing, to a fatalistic sense that puny efforts by puny humans to direct the behavior of anyone, including children, is a waste of time. Children will follow their paths as written by the One Beyond and no amount of family influence will change that. Parents, grandparents, aunts, uncles, cousins, siblings, and others in the child's life can only attempt to distract children from potentially dangerous acts; they cannot forbid or direct behaviors. Kurtz (1992) notes that parents or other child-rearing adults will offer sweets to children who might be preparing to run into a busy street as a temptation to avoid harmful behaviors. If the child is successfully distracted (and most of them usually are), clearly that was his karma.

Hindu child-rearing methods and values demonstrate an exquisite sensitivity to others around the child. Those responsible for a child's welfare—as noted, this universe is a wide one—demonstrate significant empathy to a child's emotional state. Rather than insisting that a child express herself, her emotions, her thoughts, and so forth (the American style), Indian child-rearers rely on their abilities to "read" a child. Interdependency, dependency, and group affiliation are important; autonomy and independence are not. Indians expect relatively conflict-free relationships with more diffuse boundaries between self and other. Although direct conflict is rarely displayed, when it does occur it is experienced as quite threatening. Indians will agree even if they don't agree, and they tend to deny, suppress, or contain anger. Anger is understood by Indians as dangerous to harmonious relationships and must be avoided if emotional intimacy is to be preserved. Roland argues that Hindu emotional life largely takes place internally and is not shared with one's intimates (1988).

It should be noted that Roland's view is a typically Freudian one. He assumes that emotions cannot be ignored; experience of emotion without expression of emotion, for him, is a psychological harm. Not all anthropologists would agree with this outlook (though many do). Unni Wikan, an anthropologist of Bali, demonstrates that it is indeed possible, culturally logical, and not necessarily a bad thing, to be aware of emotional reactions without expressing them (Wikan 1990). The American (and probably more generally Western) notion that one's psyche is like a hydraulic cylinder does not obtain cross-culturally (hydraulic because the view is that emotions must be expressed, and not just experienced, in one way or the other or else the psyche will blow up from too much "pressure"). Again, we see this in India (and, it should be noted, many other societies).

Personal emotional expression must be subsumed for the good of the group in India; most often that group is the extended family but it could include school, work, or friendship networks as well. By focusing on oneself, the cultural logic goes, one is ignoring the needs of others. At the same time, emotions are communicated in subtly complex ways, so that Indians in intimate relationships know when anger is about to explode, so that it can be dealt with before it emerges. Indians seem quite attuned to each other's emotional state, through a heightened ability to intuit another's feelings through a close and probably almost unconscious constant scrutiny.

This makes sense when we think about the notion of "intuition," or more specifically what in the West is known as "women's intuition," which is of course not gender related but power oriented. Those with less power in a relationship or in a society learn from the beginning how to pick up on the feelings of those in superior positions. Indians are taught from childhood how to intuit others' feelings, not just the emotions of the more powerful but the less powerful as well. There is a delicate balancing of relationships among Indians, so that even those with less power in the social hierarchy are able to make subtle demands from the more powerful. This skill means that Indians are able to take care of a concern in a relationship without anything having to be said, demonstrating a mutual but not identical interdependency.

Women, though not necessarily only mothers, are the ones who begin to foster this dependency. Through a largely nonverbal strategy, women teach children how to be proper Indian children. They provide a good deal of physical contact, and children are rarely left alone.

Indian social patterns demonstrate a deep-seated belief that persons are not meant to be independent. Children may sleep with their mothers for a number of years; after that, they likely will sleep with siblings or other relatives. Separation and aloneness are bad; dependence and interdependence are good. Also, children are always around. India in some ways could be understood as a very child-centered society: if parents go out to dinner at another family's house, children come along. There isn't the separation of adult and childish spheres that westerners seem to make (sort of; though in some ways the United States is very child-centered [cf. Bly 1996; Postman 1994], in other ways we are quite hostile to children's needs). Rather, children belong to the group and as such are seen as a natural part of it. Indeed, mothers and other child-rearers don't tend to see children as anything exceptional or delightful. Most Indians have grown up in large extended-family households, where they have had responsibility for looking after younger children. Indians, growing up, have seen children be born, get sick, die, or grow up, and, in short, have had a good deal of experience with children. Children, therefore, are nothing particularly special or interesting to most Indians. But they do need to learn how to work well within the extended family. Mothers in particular will work hard to guide a child away from her and into the extended family.

A mother will tend to respond to a child's demands fairly readily, although she will slow down the response time as the child becomes older. So, for instance, breastfeeding and weaning are rather gradual processes. A mother will provide the breast to a crying infant usually rather quickly; at the same time, however, she is aiming to push the child away from an exclusive relationship with her and into a strong identification with the family group. Feeding on cue (as Meredith Small [1998: 183–184] prefers to call it over the rather negative "feeding on demand") is standard practice; but the child usually has to make the demand over and over again until its wish is granted. So a child may cry for the breast; the mother, engaged in other activities, may ignore the cry for five minutes or so. She then will provide the breast—but she won't allow the child there for long. This means that the child will want to feed again rather quickly (and this seems to be the ideal breastfeeding pattern, according to Small [1998: 187–190], since it ensures constant high-fat milk production). The child's cries again will be likely ignored for a little bit, then she will be provided the breast, but only briefly.

A piece of Indian breastfeeding practices reflects an Indian child-rearing pattern of bargaining and its relation to belonging to the group. An Indian mother increasingly refuses her child's demands for the breast, but she eventually gives in. The message seems to be: members of the group know how to sacrifice their pleasure for the greater good, and that sacrifice in itself is rewarding. If you are to be a good member of the group, you need to learn how to stifle yourself. You'll get fed, eventually, because you're a member of the group; but you'll get more food and more respect if you abandon the breast. The child, meeting the implicit spirit of bargaining that the mother is attempting to teach, says, okay, I'll think about it, but give me the breast first. What this means is that, as the child matures, he begins to see the pleasures inherent in respect from the family group after first trying harder and harder to get the breast. By acting more maturely, the child is gratified through full membership in and honor from the group. So while an Indian mother will answer her child's demands for food, this often occurs grudgingly and with a set of conditions attached. Mothers frequently dislike the constant demands their children make on them and will hesitate to give in too quickly—her way of showing her child the path to proper mature behavior. That is, the mother is ultimately always available to the child to breastfeed but at the same time she also suggests that such demands for gratification are immature and unacceptable. The child, at his own pace, gradually acquiesces and over a period of time, controlled by the child, abandons the breast. The child ends the transitory, impersonal pleasures of nursing for the sake of more satisfying participation in the life of the family. Giving up the breast then becomes the child's voluntary sacrifice for the larger good of the family group—the value the mother is attempting to demonstrate (Kurtz 1992; Roland 1988).

Mothers adopt a business-like stance toward their children. Kids cannot expect that mothers will play with them or be easy with them. Instead, often it is grandparents—usually the mother's mother- or father-in-law—who lighten up on the discipline. Grandparents have the final word, so children can find comfort and affection from them—not from their parents. Pleasurable interaction seems mainly to take place between extended family members and the child, not between the parents and the child. This is heightened by a strong cultural prohibition on parents showing affection or laxity toward their children when grandparents or other older relatives are around. Since older relatives are quite often around, the parent-child relationship (whether mother or father) is emotionally distant in contrast to relationships in the wider family context. Mothers and fathers are culturally prohibited from demonstrating overt pride in their children, or showing clear affection or emotional intimacy, which means that emotional satisfaction is met by the wider family group, not parents (Kurtz 1992; Roland 1988).

So older relatives may tease younger children in ways not available to parents. The "give and take" game is a good illustration. Older relatives may give a child something to play with and then ask for it back not much later, using kinship terms to make the claim. If the child returns the toy, he is praised for recognizing the importance of kinship over individual wants, for giving over taking. If the child keeps the toy, he may be praised—though less often—for understanding that he has a right to the family's resources (Kurtz 1992: 79–80).

Toilet training is also marked by identification with the group. Indians neither praise children for successful training nor punish them for mistakes. Children instead tend to almost train themselves, through a combination of observing and imitating what other, respected family members do. If a child does make a mistake in the house, she will not be shamed but she may be made to feel that she is being inconsiderate of others. If the child is not trained by age five, peer pressure takes over and group teasing pressures a child to train herself (Kurtz 1992).

A mother then is trying to push the child away from her and toward the family group; at the same time, the family group is pulling the child toward it. Kurtz (1992: 77) notes that "[t]he emotional sustenance of the group acts to draw the Indian child away from the physical pleasures of his infantile attachment to the mother, prompting him to sacrifice those pleasures in return for a more mature stance within the family at large." Indian children have a different kind of relationship with their mothers than do westerners, then. Mothers don't necessarily deny the breast, or worry overly about toilet training; they know that the extended family, the group, will pull the child toward more mature behaviors (Kurtz 1992). Normal child development in India then requires a strong attachment by the child to the family group, with a denial of gratification and pleasure, for a larger, longer-term reward and pleasure—that of belonging to the extended family with all its rights and rewards.

What we see in this discussion of Indian child-rearing practices, then, is a clear set of cultural beliefs and behaviors that urge a child toward dependence on a larger, extended family. This of course creates a different set of behavioral, emotional, and cognitive patterns about how to live one's life, what one can expect from others, and how one should regard oneself than we see in the United States. American child-rearing practices are aimed, in contrast, at autonomy, independence, authentic emotional experience and expression, and intensely intimate relationships with only a very small number of people.

American child-rearing and individualism

Pretty much every message we give our children creates and maintains the American cultural insistence on individualism. Due in large part to our very low infant (and maternal) mortality rate, we have the ability to become emotionally involved with our infants; it could be argued that Americans have become emotionally involved with fetuses. This is of course not possible in other societies (Hrdy 1999; Scheper-Hughes 1993), especially those with appalling high infant mortality rates. It would be emotional suicide to become attached to a child who has a 50% chance of living until his third birthday. In the United States, such a death would be a great tragedy; in many other societies, it is a way of life. Infant mortality is a clear reflection of cultural understandings and subsequent economic conditions; there is little "natural," and almost nothing instinctive, about parental emotional engagement with children (Hrdy 1999). Yet Americans continue to insist that somehow parenting is a completely biological activity with all kinds of instincts and "natural" emotions. Americans maintain that all children "need" certain kinds of interactions, yet we deny the most fundamental ones.

For instance, Americans believe that children must learn how to stand on their own two feet. We are highly uncomfortable with children in bed with us. Indeed, the American Consumer Product Safety Commission continually issues hysterical warnings about the epidemic of deaths in the past ten years resulting from co-sleeping. That epidemic consisted, by 1999, of just over 500 deaths in a decade (CPSC 1999). Contrast this with the number of children killed in car crashes *every year*; the number is close to 10,000. The CPSC does not issue immediate warnings to keep children out of cars, despite the appalling numbers of deaths. Clearly, Americans have trouble with co-sleeping but not with automobiles—despite the fact that children develop best by sleeping with older people (parents and, later, siblings), by being able to breastfeed when they want to, by learning how to breathe, by having skin-to-skin contact, and other evolutionary and physiological needs (Small 1998).

Some of the most important things we can do for children, to prevent Sudden Infant Death Syndrome (SIDS), to provide the best nutrition possible, and to help physiological development, are condemned by American society. Parents insist that children should sleep, alone, in a separate room. The fact that children in American society typically have their own sleeping quarters, in their own rooms, is an American artifact—middle class parents, anyway, can afford large enough houses to provide separate rooms for each child whether it's truly best for the child or not. A child crying at bedtime "has to learn" how to fall asleep by herself. The child's pitiable sobs, so easily ended by simply picking her up, would "spoil" the six-month-old, according to most Americans.

And this makes sense in terms of American culture. We insist, very early on, that children "need" to be independent. In point of fact, *we* need our children to be independent; there is nothing biologically necessary about independence for children (or adults, for that matter). Instead, it is a cultural demand. Capitalism, with its competitiveness, its demands for geographic mobility, its self-absorption and selfishness, requires that family ties remain fragile and easily breakable. Capitalism, at least on the massive American scale, denies basic human needs for interdependence. An extended family organization cannot work with American capitalism. As a result, numerous myths have emerged, encouraged by our history, about independence and self-reliance in American culture. It is not surprising that those myths direct our behavior from birth, including those regarding the dangers of co-sleeping.

While there are many justifications to abandon co-sleeping, none of them hold much water. The few children who have died as a result of co-sleeping generally speaking have been smothered; a simple solution is to put the parents' bed on the floor without headboards, bedframes, or other smothering hazards. But rather than sensible recommendations, Americans' discomfort with children in bed with adults prevents what is a necessary activity. Anthropologist Meredith Small (1998) speculates that part of the discomfort may come from the association of sexual activity with a marital bed; it is not a neutral, family place but one of sexuality. Americans quite oddly are terrified of children being exposed to sexual activity (certainly this is not the case in many societies, nor is it likely to be a fear engendered by evolutionary pressures) and also seem to believe that sexual activity is infectious. The marital bed, a place of sex, cannot be any other place for family members. Certainly this is a very strange set of beliefs; we don't hold them about violence, when the empirical information is quite clear that violence is far more infectious than sexual activity.

Sexuality also becomes a focus in American child-rearing when we consider the American discomfort with breastfeeding. The empirical evidence is quite clear: infants do best with breast milk. While there are outlandish—and typically American—claims about the intellectual superiority of breastfed children, what cannot be denied is the importance of anti-biotical colostrum and high-fat breast milk for the physical well being of children. Breastfeeding was essentially eliminated as a "modern" option in the 1950s (Eyer 1992: 175), though hints of its primitive nature were extant for many decades before the cold war. After all, it was ignorant peasant immigrant women who breastfed; modern American women should not subject themselves to such a dirty and unhygienic practice (the long-standing European tradition of wet nurses for the elite is a precursor as well). In addition, the takeover of obstetrics and gynecology by men at the turn of the twentieth century, as male doctors drove midwives out of what the men saw as a highly financially rewarding field (Eyer 1992), was paralleled by a growing interest in Freudian theory.

In this scheme, breastfeeding was far too sexualized an activity and therefore inappropriate for mother and child. Though the eroticization of the breast is a peculiarly American cultural practice, its sexualized nature was not questioned by self-proclaimed men of science. Again, America's odd views of sexuality—both Puritanically horrified as well as constantly underfoot—come to the fore in breastfeeding. Because breastfeeding typically is a pleasurable—though not necessarily a sexual—experience for mothers, it was suspect. Americans, aided by Freud, seemed to believe that pleasure of any kind was, at its heart, sexually motivated and therefore bad, especially as children should not, in the American view, be exposed to sexuality of any kind. This is so largely because, as Freud said, human sexuality is a constant pressure. Americans seem to believe that the less encouragement of sexuality the better, particularly for children. The sight of a woman breastfeeding apparently will drive men mad with desire, and it almost constitutes sexual abuse for children, whether they are the recipient of breast milk or merely observing their younger sibling feeding. Once again, though, the American belief in the infectious nature of sexuality does not make sense, finally, at least when considering biological imperatives.

Americans reject co-sleeping, and we reject breastfeeding. At last count, fewer than 25% of European American women breastfeed their children at all, and the percentage of African-American women is even lower. Few families identify themselves as co-sleepers. Those who do are sometimes punished by their states' family services agencies. Although an unusual case, in Illinois in July 2000 a mother was sanctioned for breastfeeding and co-sleeping with her five-year-old son (Heneghan 2001). She was accused of sexual abuse of her child; her child was put in foster care and she was forced to take parenting lessons. The actual picture remains rather murky. Some reports alleged that she forced her child to breastfeed over his objections; others indicated that she slept in the nude with her child. Both reports were enough to raise major alarms at Illinois' Department of Children and Family Services. The assumption, unchallenged, clearly was that a five-year-old child should not see his mother's breasts, much less her nude body. There were no allegations that she actually fondled her child; apparently the alleged sight of a nude mother was enough to send social workers into a frenzy of Freudian passion. There is no biological evidence that the sight of naked people will harm a child. It is a cultural artifact.

While the above discusses an extreme case, it should be clear by now that American discomfort with sexuality, sensuality, and nudity strongly shape our child-rearing practices. The denial of basic physiological needs of infants—a need to co-sleep, a need for skin-to-skin contact, a need for breastfeeding—is a fundamental fact of American life. We provide children with precisely what they do not need—aloneness, separateness, "independence." We rear some very lonely children who come to understand that they cannot relax. They must monitor themselves since no one will do it for them.

This leads, in my view, to the current state of American culture. We are a society of self-declared independent individuals. Those of us who are baby boomers have spent our lives dwelling in therapy-speak. We constantly have our fingers on our emotional pulse, and we have taught that to our children. We do not say "I think"; we say "I feel." To deny our feelings is a bad thing; to assess others' reactions, and find them wanting, is to be judgmental, itself apparently a bad thing. Americans are self-absorbed, apparently believing that all problems can be solved with the right kind of emotional expression with the right kinds of people (therapists first, and then family members, who are just waiting to be able to tell everyone else how they feel about something). This constant yammering about feelings, rather than ideas or anything else even remotely interesting, wastes time and money and is essentially unnecessary. American society is no better off now that it has prescribed therapy for every single social and personal issue than it was before, when everything was supposedly repressed.

The American cultural focus on emotional expression can be clearly traced to our strong ideas about individualism. Chapter 2 explores these intertwined ideas more thoroughly. Many societies are far more worried about violence; yet Americans blithely expose children to violence without thinking about it. As noted before, most evidence seems to indicate that violence is far more damaging to children (and adults, for that matter) than sexuality. Yet we allow children to consume violence heedlessly. We are indeed a culture of violence.

How do we explain the rash of massacres in American middle class schools, enacted by children? (Of course, we have ignored inner-city teen murders for more than a decade. It's more frightening when "our" children do it.) In part, we talk about family breakup, the decline in values, violence in the various media, the ready availability of guns, and so forth; but what do we think caused the violence at its basis? Largely, we talk about troubled children with low impulse control and low self esteem who really must be nuts when you come down to it. The families of the teenagers are not put on trial (if they are still alive); society is not jailed; the media continue on. This seems to indicate that a basic belief we hold about behavior is that it is initiated by an individual with more or less free will, and that individual should reap the consequences of that behavior, even if it's caused by mental illness. (None of this is to say, by the way, that there isn't free will, or that there isn't a "mind" that is separate from the "body"; we're just trying to get at American cultural beliefs about behavior. Whether such things exist of course should be open to examination.)

More simply, we can see the individualistic emphasis in answer to hypothetical questions. Why are you smiling? "Because I feel happy." Why did you shoot that person? "Because he made me mad." Why are you going to college? "Because I want to get a good job." Why do you play football? "Because I'm good at it." Or even why do you have cancer? "Because I'm a Type A personality." These are relatively impoverished responses, though I suspect they are relatively typical of Americans.

More sophisticated responses might include answers such as "I smiled because I feel happy, because when you smiled at me I felt accepted and wanted to express it." However, the individual remains the locus. If the response was "I smiled because you made me through your mind control," we would likely either laugh nervously and move away quickly or suggest a therapist. Even if the response was "I smiled because you and I have a friendship that includes an understanding that we are friendly to each other, and smiles denote friendliness, so I smiled because our friendship required it at the time," we would likely be uncomfortable with such a systemic and culturally aware explanation. No, Americans prefer to explain ourselves solely within an individualistic paradigm.

That is, we tend to believe that the self—the "ego"—is an integrated, willful, self-motivated, choice-making, bounded entity activated by some kind of inner force. This "bounded" self acts on a combination of emotions, motives, and intentions inside itself, and it can change with enough will and discipline (why else go to therapy?) If behavior, emotion, and thought are contained entirely within the individual, as we believe, then it makes sense to locate the cause, and cure, of what we believe are individual problems solely within the individuals. However, there are other ways to understand this.

The diffuse self

For instance, we could quite reasonably watch phenomena beyond the individual and look for clues for behavior in—for example—family interaction, or class position, or community. Much of family systems therapy theory concentrates on trying to understand behavior from a larger point of view, seeing the causes, and the cure, for abnormal behavior in family or community life. However, family therapy—in addition to being ineffective (Epstein 1995: 93)—tends to be experienced as "blaming" by the family, especially the more functional ones. This makes sense in the context of American exaggerated individualism. These days, serious mental illness is not even treated with family therapy but with family education, if, indeed, the family is included at all (Throop 1992). Americans tend to reject explanations for behavior that tap into larger systems, unlike most people in the world.

In India, as an example, psychological anthropologists have established that South Asians construct their senses of self, identity, and motivation quite differently than do Americans. While, as I've noted, Americans tend to see ourselves as an "I" separate from "you," South Asians tend to think in terms of "we." Anthropologists have called this sense of the self the "we-self," the sociocentric self, the holistic self, or the allocentric self, among other terms. The strong sense of firm boundaries that we have about ourselves and our identities (the "bounded self" discussed by Geertz [1975]) is not shared by Indians. South Asians have a constant sense of "we-ness," not a separateness per se. They think of themselves in relation to others in their very hierarchical society. Generally, it is relationships and permeability of relationships that are valued by Indians as they constantly monitor each other for clues to the workings of their relationships (Throop 1992, 1997; Roland 1988; Kurtz 1992). It certainly is so that Americans do not think this way and indeed might find the child-rearing practices that help shape such identities to be strange and probably unhealthy (if we compare Indian child-rearing practices to American expert advice on children). Regardless, the Indian example is just one of many that demonstrates some very different constructions of self-in-society, but it is not shared by Americans.

American hyperindividualism

In contrast, the self in current American dominant culture continually is reduced to smaller and smaller concentrations of motivation and behavior, especially behaviors and emotions that we read as problematic. I call this pattern *hyperindividualism*—the cultural insistence that *all* behavior is ultimately reducible to individual motivation, whether it be intrapsychic or, more frighteningly, genetic. Complex series of culturally shaped actions are being reduced to simply physiological responses—the ultimate in individualism (hence hyperindividualism). Social structural or systemic discussions of social problems are excoriated as escapes from responsibility for perpetrators of disvalued behaviors (e.g., welfare recipients, criminals [especially juvenile offenders], "multiculturalists," feminists, poorly performing students, the mentally ill and the mentally not feeling so good [e.g., the culture of recovery, or the worried well, or what Bellah et al. {1985} refer to as the language of therapy]). People find themselves in difficult situations because they themselves (and only they themselves) are difficult; class, race, or gender are no longer salient in larger American discourse (if they ever really were). (Of course, some scholars continue to argue for the inclusion of these topics, but we are by and large marginalized in the general cultural discussion, though there are encouraging signs just lately of a broader analysis.)

Therapy then is the only solution. It is an impoverished one, to say the least.

Chapter 2

Psychotherapy and Hyperindividualism

American society relies on psychotherapy and its language to discuss and solve social problems. This solution, however, is an impoverished and superficial one. In this chapter, I demonstrate how psychotherapy is a logical, if unjust, American cultural practice; certainly it fits well within American understandings of individualism and personal responsibility. It has replaced religiously grounded moral structures with an ephemeral, self-involved value framework. In addition, it is clear that psychotherapy, in all of its formulations, does not solve the problems it is purported to do. In short, the American reliance on psychotherapy, psychology, psychiatry, social work, and counseling fits well within in our history and culture. It also is a profoundly immoral sham.

I feel your pain

Bill Clinton's famous utterance acts as exemplar for the triviality of American cultural discourse in the late twentieth and early twenty-first centuries. While perhaps sincerely intentioned, Clinton's engagement in the language of therapy (Bellah et al. 1985) as he spoke to African Americans personalizes, without remedy, America's horrific legacy of slavery, brutality, discrimination, prejudice, and hyperindividualism. Rather than focusing on the great injustices perpetrated by Americans on other Americans, and providing alternatives to those injustices, Clinton's remark instead provides a veneer of sensitivity to the emotional state of himself first and foremost and the emotional states of those who have been harmed by American cultural understandings. As though Clinton's feelings were relevant, Americans, particularly African Americans, bought into the language of therapy, the discourse of emotions, as providing some kind of justice. But emotions do no such thing, and how one feels about something is far less relevant than what one does—and Clinton did nothing of any substance about ethnic discrimination during his eight years as president.

Americans believe that emotional experience and expression are important, substantive, and salient to our lives. We believe that we should be free to fully experience our feelings, and we should be able to fully express them as we wish. Emotions, for us, can sometimes be more real than lived experience. Students, for instance, are being told—by parents, by other family members, by teachers, by the culture in general—that they are good and worthwhile and smart with no evidence. There is a belief—completely unsupported by any reputable evidence—that in order to do good one must feel good. In other words, we believe that there is something called "self-esteem" and that it must precede any worthwhile activity. We must experience ourselves as good and worthwhile and smart before we can *be* good and worthwhile and smart. We must have high self-esteem before we can do anything worth esteeming.

This is of course utter nonsense. As will be shown later in the chapter, there is no credible evidence that self-esteem is a prerequisite to brilliance or even hard work. It could be argued that high self-esteem mitigates against effort—why bother striving if you're fine as you are? More generally, the notion that emotional experience and expression makes for a good person or even interesting conversation is highly questionable. Rather than focusing on intellectual expression—thinking—or behavioral expression—doing—our discourse is filled with "feelings." One does not notice, however, a concomitant heightening of intellectual sophistication, or even a reduction in suffering, with America's increasing focus on feelings. Instead, American cultural discussions devolve further and further into infantilized talk about personal interiority.

The logic of the talk of feelings goes something like this. I experience an emotion—it could be a pleasant emotion, but it's just as likely to be an unpleasant one, such as anger or sadness. Because I am "entitled" to my feelings, I don't have to suppress the feeling. Indeed, it is part of my job as an "emotionally healthy" person to fully experience the feeling and share that feeling with you. It is your responsibility, then, to listen and respond with empathy to my feeling state. You then get to talk about how you feel about my feelings. Then I talk about how I feel about your feelings about my feelings, and so on, until either I feel better, or you feel worse, or, possibly both. Such is the scintillating conversation of the early twenty-first century.

One thing you may not do, under penalty of social ostracization, is tell me that my feelings are wrong, or bad, or inappropriate. My feelings are my feelings; I cannot "help" the way I feel. As a result, my feelings, regardless of their content, are always fine and cannot be judged. Feelings happen to me; I cannot change them. I cannot "choose" my feelings. If I am sad, I cannot choose not to be sad. I can "cover it up," perhaps, or not talk about it. But if I'm sad, I'm sad. To say I'm not sad when I am smacks, to Americans, of inauthenticity, which is a bad thing apparently. The self-help gurus, building on and expanding psychotherapeutic theory (such as it is; see Epstein 2006) only slightly, encourage us to express our genuine feelings. Feelings can't hurt anyone, say the psychotherapists. Indeed, only with the true expression of authentic affect states can true healing take place.

Also, I am the expert on myself. Unless you are specially trained as a psychotherapist, you cannot help me. Only a psychotherapist can tell me, better than I can myself, how I feel about something. My friends, meaning well, probably project their feeling states on me, and they interpret my emotions through their own lenses. As such, they are not particularly helpful. It is only the psychotherapist who can see me objectively and thus help me. Psychotherapy allows me to express myself completely, fully, and cathartically, in ways that friends—those emotionally needy amateurs—will not tolerate except in small doses, at least until all of them have been in therapy too and understand how to listen nonjudgmentally. (Woe betide the psychotherapy client who refuses to express herself emotionally!)

It is hard to see how emotionally expressive American society of the twenty-first century is any happier, more healed, or emotionally healthier than America of previous centuries. Indeed, it appears to me that we have harmed ourselves mightily by the insistence of psychotherapy and the discourse of emotions, requiring us to talk about ourselves incessantly. By demanding a constant emotional pulse-taking, any opportunity for shared intellectual, political, or other non-emotional discussions is bypassed in favor of concentrating on oneself. Furthermore, the demand for moral, intellectual, and emotional neutrality has damaged American culture badly. We have become a society of overly sensitive whiners who believe that happiness is not only attainable but a basic human right.

Happiness and privilege

This belief is so enormously ethnocentric, born of privilege and arrogance, that it is hard to know where to begin. Few societies sanction the kinds of self-interest that American psychotherapy promotes. This is in part because people in few other societies have the time to examine themselves as thoroughly as Americans do. The kind of self-monitoring and self-examination suggested by psychotherapy, both in the therapy room and outside of it, simply cannot take place in subsistence-level societies (and most societies in the world are subsistence-level). To focus on oneself rather than the needs of others could very well mean the difference between eating and not eating—that day, that week, that month, that year. Indeed, most societies across the world with any exposure to American culture understand Americans as appallingly selfish and childish to be so focused on themselves and not on others. Our independence, our (illusory) "self-reliance," our continual attention to individual needs is understood in other societies as infantile and unrealistic.

If we return for a few moments to Indian society, the point is illustrated well. Most Indians, as was discussed in chapter 1, experience themselves as a part of large and varied networks of people. The chimeras of independence and self-reliance have little place in the lives of most Indians. They realize that enmeshment in extended families, friendship networks, and workplace groups are a crucial part of survival. Rather than insisting, as do Americans, that it is right and good and proper and "natural" to stand on one's own two feet, Indians, with exquisite sensitivity, comprehend that human existence is a social endeavor. South Asians may not call on physiological or scientific explanations for their behavioral, intellectual, and—it must acknowledged—emotional cultural stances of orientation to the group. However, they are correct: there is clear evidence that humans are social beings.

Humans evolved in groups, not as separate stand-alone units. The anthropological evidence is overwhelming on this point. Hunting, gathering, fire-making, child-rearing, birth, death, eating, and all other human activities took place in groups of people, kin and non-kin. We evolved as cooperative networks, not competitive individuals. There was no such being as "Man the Hunter." Most likely, it was "Men and Women, the Hunters and Gatherers." The entire American myth of the beauty and naturalness of competition and individualism, supposedly proven out by the fossil record and the naïve recreations of "evolutionary psychologists," supports American culture but has little to do with reputable evidence. Why is it that psychological thinkers of so many different stripes are so blind to their ethnocentrism?

Well, for one thing, psychology appears to be one of the few academic disciplines almost immune from serious criticism. To even raise questions about the intellectual integrity of psychology is to provoke hostility verging on the cries of blasphemy from some psychologists. Any discussion of the moral vapidity of psychology and the various forms of psychotherapy appears to paint the discussant as so conservative as to be reactionary, and probably in need of some serious psychotherapy. Psychology, in American culture, is not challenged, while most other social sciences have been roundly criticized externally and internally. What makes psychology so dominant, so able to repel even questions about its utility?

An obvious answer, of course, is that the value systems of psychology and, more specifically, psychotherapy, cooperate quite well with American hyperindividualism. As we will see in later chapters, this certainly is true from public policy perspectives. If recipients of American social services as required by social policy are largely responsible for their predicaments—and this is indeed how they are painted—then individualistic solutions (therapy, jobs, jail, foster care, etc.) are the only logical ones. And psychotherapists are happy to provide those social services. Psychotherapy does not force Americans to take hard looks at themselves, their privileges, their luxuries, their moralities. Psychotherapists argue that the world will be a better place when we all are enlightened about ourselves, when we have insight, when we all have high self-esteem. Rarely do they argue that it may be useful to provide a more equitable economic system, for instance (so that, perhaps, a garbage collector makes as much as a therapist). No, what we need to do is understand everyone's pain; there are even therapists these days who help people feel good about having too much stuff. God forbid that a wealthy person should be judged selfish (after all, who pays the psychologist's bills?).

Psychotherapy has created, or at least maintained, an American cultural belief in selfishness. If a person is concerned with the needs of others, she is co-dependent—and that's bad, apparently. Making moral choices based, perhaps, on values of social justice that could mean the individual is harmed in some way is seen as unhealthy emotionally. We are only responsible for ourselves, say the therapists. We can't really take care of anyone else. We don't create other people's feelings. We can hardly manage our own. We have no imperative to care much about others if those others are hampering our own freedoms and feelings. Psychotherapists pride themselves on being nonjudgmental and neutral. It is plain that psychotherapy is simply dripping with moral evaluations.

That's where happiness comes in. It is, apparently, principle number one of the psychotherapists' credo, that happiness is attainable, desirable, and an essential right of all humans. This is a clear moral statement. Moral statements in all societies aver what is good and what is bad. The morality of psychotherapy includes the basic belief that happiness is good and unhappiness is bad. Furthermore, the only way to be happy is to be independent, to take responsibility for yourself and your feelings (but not for anything else). No one "makes" you feel in any particular way; you feel that way. No one "makes" you behave in any particular way (though it has to be said that psychotherapy cares very little about behavior in and of itself, with a few exceptions like structural and strategic family therapy and behavioral therapy, both of which are largely rejected by mainstream psychotherapy); unlike feelings, you choose to behave in certain ways. But what's important is how you feel about your behavior.

How your behavior affects anyone else is largely irrelevant to psychotherapists. Hurting other people's feelings, hampering other people's lives, annoying others, inconveniencing others, even actually physically harming other people all can be explained, in the logic of psychotherapy, through an examination of emotions. And since emotions are, in this logic, value-free, apparently simply just *are*, they cannot be judged as good or bad. They can, perhaps, be "managed" (see chapter 4 for a discussion of "anger management"); indeed, as pointed out in chapter 1, there has been an effort on the part of Americans to manage most of emotional life until recently. But even those efforts focus on the self.

Americans quite simply reject the notion that they are embedded in networks of behavior. A fundamental principle of structural and strategic family therapy is that emotion, thought, and behavior are, by and large, constructed through interaction (Minuchin 1974, 1981 [for instance]; Haley 1982). Interiority is flexible and reactive rather than fixed and initiating in this set of systems theories. What is most important to systems theorists is behavior, and more specifically sequences of behavior. How a particular family member feels is not especially relevant to the psychotherapeutic process; what counts is how she acts. Therapy sessions are built around attempts to modify patterns of interaction within the family group. Unfortunately, but not too surprisingly, family therapy is no more effective than any other kind of psychotherapy (Epstein 1997: 114). Epstein remarks that this could be partly because the treatment unit—a small group, the family—is too small for lasting treatment (ibid.). It also seems likely that family therapy, and the principles and assumptions behind it, challenge cherished American cultural understandings about self-reliance and individual responsibility as well as more recent cultural ideals that permit emotional exploration of the self in ways that aggressively counter effective social interaction.

The American focus on self begins early. There has long been a folk belief that American infants are born with a "personality" that remains relatively fixed throughout their lifetimes. That is, we think that children come out at least somewhat prepackaged, with characteristically idiosyncratic responses and desires that differ, to some extent, from child to child, and those responses and desires are evident pretty much from birth. While we pay attention to child development experts and their charts and percentiles, we truly believe that every single child is unique, special, and fascinating. It is every parent's responsibility, we think, to provide nurturing environments that will allow the child to fully develop into the person he already is.

Psychologists help to promote this myth. There are six clear personality types, according to these "experts" (Downey 2000: E1, E3), for instance. They offer no evidence that these types have been scientifically established. Instead, they encourage parents to listen for the child's feelings and respond accordingly. The advice provided by psychologists for parents of children read like astrology predictions: for the "Feelers," for instance, children who apparently "view their world through emotions," the proper parent will "avoid direct questions or giving orders" (E1). This is supposed to help the child feel comfortable with himself so he can develop as fully as possible.

Indeed, the entire concept of these personality types, and, in fact, just about all child development expertise, focuses on the special uniqueness of every child. In addition to its patent illogic (after all, if uniqueness is ubiquitous, then everyone is the same), it is false. Certainly we can say with a little bit of surety that all children everywhere generally go through some of the same physical stages at more or less the same time, depending on economic, social, cultural, and political conditions (in times of starvation, children develop physically rather differently than children who live in plenty. Most children live in marginal economic circumstances across the world). However, to jump from that rather established fact to outlining personality types for children is quite a stretch.

Psychologists, psychotherapists, social workers, counselors, child development experts, and so on are abundantly clear in their discussions of children. They assume a psychobiological stance. Though few, if any, of these experts have any experience in studying behavior cross-culturally, the psychologists and their colleagues confidently state their folk theories as established scientific fact. "All children need to be independent," they gaily declare. "It's part of human nature."

Human nature, in fact, is thrown about with no little carelessness by psychotherapists. Yet most have absolutely no insight into human nature. They know about American culture, to be sure, since the values of American culture are what they are spouting. However, they reject any notion that these are in fact cultural understandings. They continue to firmly believe that somehow, magically, Americans are somehow more human than people anywhere else in the world. Americans embody the values and ideal behaviors, thoughts, and emotions of psychologists. Other societies hide, cover up, or deny basic human nature, and Americans do too but not so badly.

Now, the idea that Americans—or, more generally, Western Europeans and Americans—are somehow more human, more culturally evolved, is not a new one. Even anthropologists, who study human behavior from a global rather than local perspective, have discussed other societies' cultural patterns as deficient. While the list of such naïve publications is far too long to provide here, exemplars of course would include Malinowski, Boas, Fortune, DuBois, Scheper-Hughes (who manages to produce ingeniously value-laden studies while claiming objectivity) and most ethnographers of India until recently (see Kurtz 1992 for a complete discussion of Indian ethnography) among many others. Using Freudian frameworks at first, and then other psychological theoretical structures as Freudianism faded, anthropologists have joined their psychological colleagues in judging societies different than their home culture as backward, defective, in denial, repressed, or primitive. No, anthropologists have been no better than psychologists in understanding human behavior, at least until recently.

However, a key difference in cultural anthropology has been its very nature. By living in another society for years at a time, as we do, we have been confronted with the effects of Western, and more particularly American, hubris on a day-to-day basis. We are asked to explain ourselves, our society, and our wealth. In doing so, many of us learn to see our home cultures, these days, in quite humbling lights. We have been endangered while performing our ethnographic fieldwork. We have witnessed quite different ways of living, experienced by those engaged in such activities as perfectly legitimate, rational, and logical. Once an anthropologist sees the effect of American dominant culture on those unable to purchase it, a belief in American cultural superiority becomes difficult to sustain. We have discovered the truth about cultural relativism: that there are indeed thousands of different ways of understanding the world. Until a person knows enough about enough societies, judgment must be suspended. Some of those ways are morally reprehensible, to be sure (I would include parts of American culture in that judgment). But until a person is able to take herself out of her American cultural understandings and truly attempt to experience another society's way of being, she really cannot understand much about human behavior. She might know something about American behavior, but not human nature.

And that is exactly where psychotherapists err. By blithely assuming that they are being culturally sensitive when talking about, for instance, "African American culture," they think they are being cross-cultural. But they are not, for several reasons. For one thing, there is no such thing as "African American culture." African Americans, like all groups within the United States, conform remarkably to American dominant culture. For some African Americans it is a matter of coercion—if they do not act like middle class European Americans, their children may remain in foster care forever. For others, American dominant culture resonates strongly with economic and social aspirations. In what else is the fury of young African American men based when they respond to disrespect? Disrespect indicates being treated as less than a valuable individual—a cornerstone of American hyperindividualism.

African American parents and their children are enmeshed in dominant culture through the educational system, the medical system, the welfare system, and the economic system more generally, through the electronic media, through religion. The current focus in education on self-esteem (as opposed to actually learning something) means that children in predominantly African American schools learn about "their culture," usually an appalling mishmash of widely varying African societies. They learn this so they can be proud to be African American. This is, of course, a legitimate goal, but the incredible simplemindedness of something like "Kwaanza," for instance, encourages African Americans to remain ignorant of the diversity of African cultures.

The medical system, particularly pediatrics, also helps to keep African Americans within American dominant culture. Americans' touchingly sweet belief that pediatricians actually know something about children's behavior infects African Americans as well as other Americans. As noted before, child development experts argue that children are unique, and special, and wonderful; children also are meant to fall into various ranges and percentiles for behavior.

African American parents are subject to those charts and ranges as much as are other American parents. If a child does not seem to be developing along the charts, doctors begin to get suspicious (it has only been lately that charts based on the major ethnicities in the United States have been developed; until recently, the standard was European American male as it has been for just about everything). If parents do not seem that interested in their children, doctors become suspicious. If children are underweight or overweight, according to the charts, doctors get suspicious. Oh, yes, African Americans are subject to American dominant culture just as much as other Americans.

African American parents understand, and generally agree, that children are unique and wonderful and special. They are just as concerned for their children's equal treatment in school as are other American parents. They fight for their children's right to education. They demand appropriate resources for their children. They require that their children be treated with dignity and respect. If their children need medical treatment or medication, they do their best to obtain it. In other words, African American parents tend to hold the same beliefs and values about children as do all Americans. It is highly unlikely that there is a separate culture of child-rearing, or even a separate culture in general, for African Americans. At most, it is a variation, also shared by many poor European American, Latino/Latina, and Asian parents, in which extended or expanded family plays a larger role in child-rearing than it does among middle-class European Americans. It appears that economic position, far more than some separate "culture" tied to a specific ethnicity, has more to do with behavioral patterns.

However, many psychotherapists insist otherwise. If the discourse of therapy did not control so much of American life, their naiveté would be amusing. Sadly, therapists determine much of what happens in this culture, and we have bought it wholesale, even in the face of its rampant ineffectiveness and immorality.

Psychotherapy's failure

Put baldly, psychotherapy simply does not work. A brave handful of scholars have challenged the dominant American paradigms of hyperindividualism and psychotherapeutic discourse. For instance, professor of social work William Epstein, at the University of Nevada-Las Vegas, has analyzed the major studies in psychology that purport to demonstrate the great effectiveness of psychotherapy in easing human suffering (1995, 1997, 2006). Epstein's analysis very clearly indicates that psychotherapy does not solve the problems it claims to do. It is not simply that one or the other school of psychotherapy is more or less effective. *Psychotherapy, as a cultural process, does not work*. Epstein demonstrates that both psychotherapy clients as well as members of control groups, in follow-up interviews ranging from six months to two years after intervention, show no difference. That is, those who receive therapy and those who do not have the same outcome. Sometimes that outcome is positive, from the point of view of the individual, and sometimes it is negative. But therapy makes no difference to their life outcomes.

Epstein argues that this astounding result is swept under the American cultural rug for a number of reasons. His most significant analysis centers around what he terms "social efficacy." For Epstein, Americans choose to believe in psychotherapy because it does not require us to expend resources on solutions to problems that would be more expensive. That is, in comparison to a massive reorganization of the American economy so that wealth is distributed more fairly—which could lead to a significant reduction in human suffering for most Americans—psychotherapy is cheap. If Americans wanted to actually assist their fellow Americans, Epstein argues, we would have pushed for social policies that did so. But psychotherapy, says Epstein, provides a convenient explanation for Americans and in addition does not require us to alter our lives in any significant way. Unlike other critics of American society, Epstein does not believe that there is a ruling oligarchy determining social policy against the wishes of the American people. In essence, for Epstein, the social policy we want is the one we get.

I am not so sure. Epstein gives rather too much power to the American people, I think. By arguing that the psychotherapeutic solution is one more or less freely chosen by the electorate, he ignores the massive influence of the various media on American thought and decision making. While certainly a case can be made for a strong strain toward individualism in American culture and history (and psychotherapy, as shown in chapter 1, is a logical if unfortunate result), that cultural precept is rarely challenged by the directors of popular culture. Like Epstein, I do not believe that there is an evil cabal of policy makers rubbing hands in devilish fashion saying "let's fool the populace with psychotherapy rather than social justice." However, Americans make political—and thus policy—choices based on information available to hand, and that includes the lack of attention paid by the "talking heads" to the ineffectiveness of psychotherapy. Though not all that much of a surprise, Americans are not freely opting for psychotherapy after surveying all options. Only one option is provided by American culture, and that is the cult of hyperindividualism and the resultant solution to social problems can only be psychotherapy of one kind or another.

Yet psychotherapy, as demonstrated above, is not effective. Epstein is not the only person to think this. Certainly we can look to the enormous good works and historical influence of a number of tortured souls, such as Abraham Lincoln, Mohandas Gandhi, and Winston Churchill. We can conclude, fairly, I think, that the American cultural focus on happiness may preclude many Americans from accomplishing anything of import.

In particular, the emphasis in American society on self-esteem is, for social workers Specht and Courtney (1994), just plain silly. Specht and Courtney examine the empirical evidence on programs focusing on self-esteem for both youngsters and adults and find them wanting. There is no evidence whatsoever that encouraging people to have positive self-regard prior to positive, useful behavior is useful in any way. Indeed, Specht and Courtney, in an examination of the California Task Force on Self-Esteem's report (1994: 50–59), uncover major methodological problems and serious misstatements of the results of psychological research. For instance, they note that the entire report downplays the fact that self-esteem seems to have absolutely no affect on behavioral outcomes and instead recommends a myriad of programs and social policies aimed at enhancing Californians' self-esteem (55). It appears that a person's self-esteem levels have no influence on academic performance, sexual activity, susceptibility to drug or alcohol use, teenage pregnancy, use of public welfare funds, child abuse, and homelessness (50–59). How someone feels about her worth as a person is not relevant to either her socioeconomic position or her behavior. But California—and at this point the larger American culture—insist that self-esteem is the key to solving our social problems. This is true, by the way, regardless of ethnicity for the most part. Middle-class European Americans certainly believe that self-esteem is important for both adults and children, but so do African Americans, Latinos/Latinas, and Asian Americans. Given that this flies in the face of objective, empirical evidence, Specht and Courtney argue that empirical evidence is not important to psychology and the other disciplines involved in psychotherapy despite their claims to the contrary.

Why would this be so? Here we must throw Epstein into the mix. The vast majority of Americans, regardless of ethnicity, truly believe that self-esteem is of major importance in child-rearing and psychological health. American folk beliefs, shaped (as noted before) by the various media and "experts" with whom Americans have contact as well as American historical trends, see individualistic solutions, framed by happiness, as the only appropriate one. Lack of true demonstrable efficacy is irrelevant in this set of beliefs. Like religious beliefs, the ineffectiveness of American cultural reliance on psychotherapy is explained away by ritual or personal ineptitude; the foundational belief in the usefulness of psychotherapy, however, cannot be challenged.

Psychotherapy as religion

I certainly am not the first to argue that psychotherapy has supplanted religious belief as the major moral and explanatory framework for behavior in American culture. Chriss (1999), Bellah et al. (1985), and Vitz (1977), among others, have discussed the pervasiveness of the psychotherapeutic discourse in American life. Chriss (1999: 3–5), for instance, hints at the change in American culture using a Foucaultian analysis. He argues that twenty-first century American society is a postmodern one in which substantial connections between self and other have fragmented, if not entirely dissolved. In earlier times, Chriss notes, a person was situated in networks of meaning such as neighborhood, family, school, church, and so forth (though he does not address the potentially confining nature of such networks or the effects of ethnicity, class, and gender for further confinement). Our society, it can be fairly said, does not contain such networks for many individuals lately. The rise of the therapeutocracy (Habermas's term appropriated by Chriss [1999: 3]), concomitantly with the decline of local face-to-face communities and personal networks, was, perhaps, happenstance but real nonetheless. Chriss asserts that the primacy of psychotherapy as an explanatory framework in American folk beliefs about behavior matched a pervasive alienation, if not anomie, of Americans from each other and themselves, or, more precisely, their selves. Psychotherapy stepped in to assist with self-assembly.

Now, a person could object, fairly, that psychotherapy has not supplanted religious belief in the United States. After all, our imaginary interlocutor might say, the rise of the religious right in the past thirty years or so disproves the replacement of religious belief with belief in psychotherapy. Such a protestation would be accurate, on its face. It does appear that Americans tend to be rather regular worshippers. A recent survey seems to indicate that more than 40% of Americans attend a religious service of some kind at least once a week (Newport 2007). Of course, attendance at worship services does not necessarily prove religious belief. What is more important here than religious belief, however, is the nature of religious belief being promoted.

Other than a few rigidly and unusually fundamentalist sects, most monotheistic and the few polytheistic belief systems in the United States today are therapeutic in nature. For instance, advertisements abound across the country featuring a young, handsome pastor of a pan-Christian "superchurch"; these churches buy large amounts of television ad time, especially during the local news hours. The pastor does not exhort the television viewers seeing his advertisement that going to church is the morally correct thing to do. He does not tell us that God tells us to go to church, or that the Bible should direct our lives. No, this pastor discusses how personally fulfilling is the love of Jesus Christ. Perfect happiness is available if we just open our hearts to the Lord, says he. Accepting Jesus will make us feel good about ourselves. This is an essentially therapeutic argument. The logic here is that belief in God will provide us with good self-esteem; God is the Final Therapist.

This set of beliefs, this rhetoric of happiness and therapy, is not limited of course to superchurches. Most American religions today are focused on messages of eternal bliss, love, comfort, and caring supposedly offered by a belief in some kind of Christian (or Judeo-Christian) God (it is not clear that American Islamic or Orthodox Jewish creeds communicate the same message). Religious belief in America these days seems to be about how to find individualistic psychological fulfillment within Christianity. Indeed, one can see the importance of hyperindividualism in evangelical religious practitioners, who are exhorted and encouraged to share their belief systems with everyone they meet. "Saving" others through talking about your personal psychological self-esteem, garnered through your personal relationship with Jesus Christ, is one of the major behavioral expectations for evangelicals.

The "personal relationship with Jesus Christ" sounds suspiciously like a therapeutic one. You are supposed to be able to talk to Jesus Christ, and He will always listen. You share your worries with Him, and your fears and your dreams, and He will provide the answers you need. Those answers may not be what you want, but they will be what you, in His divine judgment, need. It is your responsibility to develop the relationship with Jesus Christ. He will be waiting but, unless you know what you're looking for, He will not initiate anything with you. Your relationship with him is one of perfect love, without sexuality. He will give unceasingly if you but ask.

What I have just outlined mimics the professional code of ethics for most disciplines involved in psychotherapeutic practice. The therapeutic relationship is meant to be one-sided: the therapist is knowledgeable, while the client comes to the therapist for that insight. The client shares fears, dreams, and worries with the psychotherapist, who listens and provides interpretations of those verbalizations whether the client agrees with the interpretations or not. Psychotherapists usually may not solicit potential clients (though often psychotherapy is used by the state coercively with less wealthy and privileged individuals and families). Psychotherapists are forbidden to engage in sexual activity with clients or former clients (though of course some do), but they are commanded to love their clients, providing unconditional acceptance of the client. Though some psychotherapists attempt to set "boundaries" for clients (not accepting after-hours calls, for instance, and not publishing their home phone numbers in the phone book), at least during the therapy session psychotherapists must pay complete and full attention to clients. The psychotherapeutic relationship is not so different than the Christian one.

Yet, as is true with prayer and other forms of religious activity, psychotherapy has been shown conclusively to be ineffective. People still believe in both, however. The explanatory framework justifying wholeheartedly support in both institutions is remarkable. Prayers are not answered, in the religious explanation, because you said the prayer wrong, or you are praying for the wrong thing, or you're praying for the right thing but at the wrong time. Never is the idea put forth that prayers aren't answered because there is no being around who answers prayers. And one would not expect that a religion would argue that its rituals are ineffective because there is no God. The first principle of all religious belief, completely untested and not verifiable, is that God (or some version thereof) exists.

Similarly, psychotherapy—I'll repeat it again—is ineffective. But the same kinds of arguments are used, when arguments are used at all, in response to criticism, when that infrequent occurrence takes place. If a client's personal situation does not improve despite the provision of psychotherapy, it is for a number of reasons. Perhaps the client is resisting the insights that the psychotherapist is providing; a huge literature on resistance, both in Freudian and other kinds of psychotherapy, has been published. Resistance to psychological truths provided by the therapist is due to the client's inability to understand those truths; or the client has constructed elaborate defenses to block out threatening psychic material; or the client simply does not want to change, and is comfortable in his misery. A client may not improve, further, because he is being offered the wrong kind of therapy. Psychologists and others in the therapy trade spend countless hours and volumes arguing over the proper therapeutic and "theoretical" approach to take to human suffering and its solution. If the client would only receive, say, family systems therapy rather than neo-Freudian object relations therapy, he would get better so fast your head would spin. Or a client doesn't improve because he is just not focused on the therapeutic encounter; he has too many other piddling issues (making a living, perhaps) that keep him from fully or even partially engaging in therapy. Again, as with religion, nowhere in the explanations for why a client does not succeed in therapy is the idea that psychotherapy does not work.

Neither religion nor psychotherapy would be so foolish as to declare that its first principles—that there is a God, or that psychotherapy is scientifically valid—are false. In this, they are unlike many other disciplines and activities that purport to explain humanity. As a result, when either religious belief or psychotherapy is challenged in twenty-first-century America, the critic is pilloried.

Religious belief, in order to be acceptable to most Americans today, has had to adopt psychotherapeutic stances. Psychotherapy, for its part, has subsumed earlier kinds of religious belief, largely those of mysticism and a belief in a powerful, omniscient being who intervenes in one's life directly (in this case, the psychotherapist). American religion has rejected, by and large, mystical ideas while psychotherapy has appropriated them (see Epstein 2006 for a different but related treatment of these ideas). In any case, serious interrogation of either kinds of belief system is frequently punished at worst, ignored at best. We critics continue on nonetheless.

Why, for instance, would a psychotherapeutic paradigm be appropriate for recipients of welfare? What is it in our history and culture that views the very poor in American society as responsible for their own fortunes (or lack of fortunes, in this case)? It is to welfare and its attendant social services that I turn next.

Chapter 3

Poverty Is Just a State of Mind

American dominant culture understands poverty as a defect of character, not a result of a structurally unjust economic system. People who are poor are not poor because they lack money. They are poor because, in America's dominant culture, there is something wrong with them emotionally, morally, subculturally, or behaviorally. People in poverty in the United States are largely viewed as individually responsible for their own economic circumstances, and they must be punished in this view (see Ryan 1976 and Schneider 1999 for representative takes on the issue). This appallingly cruel perspective has a long history in the United States despite its patent falsity, going far beyond the "blaming the victim" nonsense furthered by allegedly liberal social scientists and providers of social services (including social workers, psychotherapists, counselors, and other purveyors of the "helping" professions).

Partly because Americans believe that success and failure are individually based, we reject cultural and systemic explanations for poverty as socialist, or, worse, communist, distinctions that are nonsensical and not necessarily bad anyway. With enough hard work and grit, anyone should be able to make it, we say. Especially in a booming economy, but even in one that at the moment is faltering badly, we seem to believe that poor people are poor because they lack a good work ethic, or they have poor educational skills, or they adhere to a "culture of poverty" that prevents personal and economic progress, or they choose not to be educated, or they are lazy welfare queens. (Apparently, child-rearing, at least as practiced by poor women, doesn't count as "real" work, though I dare middle-class husbands to tell their wives that child-rearing and housewifery do not constitute work!) Charles Murray and Richard Hernnstein went so far as to say that African Americans—40% of whom remain mired in poverty presently—are genetically inferior and in fact should not aspire to even modest prosperity (Hernnstein and Murray 1994). Discussion of structural, cultural, and institutionalized racism, sexism, and classism are entirely left out of American belief systems.

The most persistent argument made about the causes of poverty—which, after all, can be defined in its entirety as a continual lack of money—is that poor people engage in and maintain a "culture of poverty." This idea, first mooted by Oscar Lewis (1959), an anthropologist working among the poor of Mexico City in the late 1950s, involved a discussion of, essentially, a present-time orientation and an inability to defer gratification (it should be noted that Lewis was horrified by how his work was decontextualized, misappropriated, and misused by social scientists and politicians and also clearly argued, as he examined poor families in Mexico, Puerto Rico, and New York, that, given the choices available to the families with whom he worked and lived, no other rational behavior was possible [Lewis 1959, 1963, 1965]).

In other words, the poor were (and are) poor because they are unable to anticipate the future and thus blow whatever money they do manage to get their hands on through hedonistic spending instead of saving it, or shopping economically instead of focusing on what they want right now. If they don't want to work, they don't work and instead rely on the government to support their bad behaviors (unmarried parenthood, drug use, laziness). If their kids are out of control, it's because they lack parenting skills and instead are focused on their own lazy desires.

The poor, in this conceptualization, are, as Ehrenreich sees it, infantilized (Ehrenreich 1990: 48–52). After all, who is unable to defer gratification? Who wants what he wants when he wants it, right now? Who relies on others to provide for them? Who cries when she doesn't get what she wants? Babies, that's who. And this how the poor continue to be treated, forty-five years after the "culture of poverty" was first discussed.

Sure, the argument today is a little more sophisticated—and a lot more angry, invoking Victorian discussions of social Darwinism as we abandon 25% of our citizens. Instead of discussing the culture of poverty as the sole reason for poverty—bad enough in itself—we now have come up with cultures of dependency, multigenerational welfare recipients teaching their children that they don't *have* to work or go to school like the rest of "us." There is the "underclass" (Auletta 1982), the supercriminal juvenile delinquent who lives without a conscience, the "superpredator" (James Q. Wilson), the drug culture, and so on. All of these have fostered individuals who are uneducated if not illiterate (in terms of reading, writing, and numbers), who have few "life" skills, and who have no motivation to "work." The poor person, in the dominant culture, remains seen as the result of personal failure. It is then the poor person who must be "fixed."

Welfare reform—in truth, the destruction of the Great Society—aims at that repair. Although lip service is made toward some structural problems—daycare and job training are the primary targets—the individual poor person has to transform herself. Our existing economic, educational, social, and cultural systems have nothing to do with the maintenance of poverty for the dominant culture. Class, race, and gender are not explanatory in dominant American culture. White male privilege is irrelevant—indeed, these folks now see themselves, amazingly, as under attack. The obscene and growing gap between rich and poor has, in this culture view, nothing to do with poverty. Instead, just as charity organization societies did in the 1860s, current social policy insists that inside the poor person is a middle-class person just busting to get out.

Another part of this policy emphasis believes, rather naively, that poor children would not be poor if their mothers would just get married. Indeed, the Heritage Foundation's Robert Rector argues that getting rid of single parenthood would eliminate most problems of poverty in the United States (Rector 2007). Nowhere, though, in Rector's analysis of American poverty is the issue of low wage work addressed. Let's think about this, though, in terms of marriage.

How would it make logical financial sense for a poor woman to marry? Who is a poor woman most likely to meet? Other poor people. It is most likely, then, that the pool of eligible marital partners for a poor woman will be a poor man (assuming he isn't in jail or the military, as many poor men are). So the conservative solution to poverty is not to provide more money but to bring two poor people together—to be poor together, I suppose (see Ehrenreich 1997 for a similar discussion).

Let's assume that this low wage couple marries, and, while we're in fantasy land, let's assume that they both have full time jobs—something available to few low wage workers. Both working forty hours a week at the minimum wage (in May 2008) of $5.85/hour will bring in, separately and before taxes, social security, and other deductions, $234 a week or not quite $1000/month. So between the two of them we can expect them to earn $1310 a month after deductions. Now, this is before health care, or daycare (if there are any children—if there is even one child this family is all of a sudden below the poverty line, and just above it without children), or transportation (car or public transport if it's available), or rent, or food, or property taxes (if they own a house), or insurance, or utilities. Generally speaking, most states won't provide welfare, a housing subsidy, or Medicaid to this couple, though food stamps might be a possibility. But the "able-bodied" are expected to provide for themselves—even when paid such appallingly low wages. How on earth is marriage supposed to be an economic advantage in a situation like this? As Barbara Ehrenreich argued in a speech some time back (1997) in order for a poor woman to be lifted out of poverty, she would have to marry at least two-and-a-half poor men. I'm guessing, though, that conservatives are not promoting polyandry. They mainly, it seems, want to be left alone to count their dugats. So it's not so clear that marriage is an adequate path out of poverty for poor women.

What about education? Is education the path to success for poor people? Yes, it is. That is very much clear. Those with a high school diploma definitely make a better living than those without one, and those with an associate's degree make more than someone with a high school diploma, and those with a baccalaureate degree make more than someone with an associate's degree. The question really is: how accessible is education to the poor? We can say with great certainty that poor people almost always go to underfunded school systems, right from the start. Even those young people who are provided Head Start programs tend to start losing ground in third grade unless their schools are well funded with low student-teacher ratios, good supplies, well-maintained buildings, well-educated teachers, an engaged school administration, an interested community, and an involved family.

Poor children and families do not have access to schools like that. By definition, poor people don't have much money and therefore do not have much to contribute via real estate taxes to their local school systems. Poverty-stricken school systems tend not to attract excellent teachers; they tend to have run-down buildings and, often, a burned-out, substandard administration consumed by serious disciplinary issues. Poor schools tend as well to have old books, if they have any at all, few supplies, and student bodies suffering from a number of maladies of the poor (lead poisoning, asthma, developmental delays, major dental issues, diabetes, and so forth). Poor schools, whether inner city or Appalachia, are not energetic bastions of challenging and insightful instruction. More often than not, poor schools teach badly right from the start.

So poverty-stricken students start from far behind. College must often seem a far away dream to many poor children. Indeed, school counselors in some parts of the United States actively discourage young people from even considering college. They participate in the oppression of those already so regularly oppressed. And, indeed, though most American young people these days are woefully underprepared for the rigors of college (see chapter 6), those who are poor are being cheated, regularly. They are being cheated by school systems that do not demand equity. They are being cheated by their legislators. They are being cheated by their families who do not insist on more. They are being cheated by their teachers who do not require a minimal standard of learning. Ultimately, of course, they are being cheated by all of us. How can they even aspire to the middle class when schooling is so devalued? We seem to want the poor to act in middle-class ways, though, despite the fact that the path is blocked.

The middle-class poor

Apparently, all we have to do is teach that person how to be middle class—how to (supposedly) control her impulses for sex, food, and sleep so that she can act and look like the rest of "us." She's resistant to middle-class values of child-rearing or the work ethic? Give her parenting classes and therapy; don't examine whether middle-class child-rearing is producing good results. She can't read? Get her a tutor; don't look at why the resources of American schools, even those that are well funded, are graduating very poorly educated young people (who nonetheless have good self-esteem, though it appears that they have done little of which to be proud). She doesn't have a good work ethic? Stick her in a program that will provide job training through humiliating, sometimes racist, and often patronizing job coaches; don't explore why a normal adult human being would refuse to work in jobs that are demeaning, degrading, and so low paid as to put her below the poverty line. She won't stop having sex and getting pregnant? Make her accept Norplant or sterilization as a condition of receiving any poverty-related government grants; don't analyze the gross sexualization—and contradictory prudishness—of American culture. She's using illicit drugs? Force her to pee in a cup and be drug-tested before being handed her humiliatingly meager TANF (Temporary Assistance to Needy Families, the most recent iteration of "welfare," altered with the welfare reform act of 1996) check. Her kids are out of control? Force her to learn how to parent "correctly" or surrender her children to the hell of foster care; don't examine how larger cultural patterns and beliefs about children are warping all notions of childhood, whether middle class or otherwise, and, in a parallel way, adulthood (Bly 1996). No, her poverty is not because she doesn't have money; she's poor because she won't act like middle-class people, even while that avenue is barred.

And, anyway, is the middle class all that different (see, e.g., Ehrenreich 1990 for a more sympathetic view)? As I write in May 2008, the housing market is in disarray and middle-class people—not just the poor and the working poor—are losing their houses. The amount of credit card debt carried by the average American hovers around $8,000 as of 2004 (Kahn n.d.: 1). The middle class spends more than it earns (ibid.). How exactly can we see this as a group of people with good impulse control?

The middle class is not exactly the best group to admire. Not only do members of this class seem unable to refrain from purchasing toys (like Wiis or iPhones); they seem unable to refrain from purchasing houses when they plainly cannot afford them. People are buying far more house than they can pay for and, indeed, they are buying houses with no down payment and no savings in the bank to cover a leaking roof or broken plumbing. Because American culture insists that grown-ups must own houses, young married couples, or even unmarried ones, are purchasing three or four bedroom homes that they cannot possibly afford.

In addition to the middle-class tendency toward profligacy in the housing market (and the associated subprime mortgages that cannot now be refinanced), we see laziness. The middle class seems to be watching more and more television (and, of course connected to this is that they are reading fewer and fewer books, magazines, and newspapers [National Endowment for the Arts 2007]). Middle-class college students, instead of actually doing research, are plagiarizing from the Internet at an alarming rate (see chapter 6)—and their parents are justifying their children's thievery!

Indeed, college students today appear resentful of having to, say, read books or write papers and, at least among my colleagues at selective liberal arts college, anecdotal evidence indicates that college students overall don't appear to actually want to concentrate or—again—write their own words. The "millennial" generation (I prefer to call this group the Trophy Generation, as they are used to being rewarded for coming in ninth place in an eight-horse race) appears to behave in ways significantly different from their parents—but see chapter 4 for a further discussion of the high self-esteem world in which the middle class (though not the poor) has been reared.

Moreover, we see the impulsive actions of the privileged when we view the sexual behavior of college students. Middle-class young people are reverting to pre-AIDS behavior as we see a drastic rise in STDs (sexually transmitted diseases) and, recently, a rise in teenage pregnancy rates again. Among young gay men, there has been a rise in the diagnosis of HIV and AIDS as those young men assume a cure will be found before they get too sick (*New York Times* 2008).

So what we can see is this: though social workers, psychologists, counselors, and others in the psychotherapeutic community urge the poor to model themselves after the middle class, I'm not so sure the middle class is the best role model right now. The same lack of impulse control attributed to the poor, the same laziness, the same difficulty handling money, the same trouble with marriage, appear in both class positions. And both are culturally constructed, transmitted, and judged.

Indeed, the latest legislative trend involves requiring welfare recipients to make themselves available for random drug testing. The reasoning seems to be that, since "they" are getting "our" money, it is "our" responsibility to make sure that "they" are not spending it on drugs. Hmm. Just about all of us receive federal monies on an individual level; if it is not through a direct cash grant, such as TANF, it is through mortgage interest deductions. I wonder how homeowners who take that deduction, in effect an income transfer from the government to the taxpayer, would feel about IRS agents showing up at random, requiring them to pee in a cup, and with a consequence of tax deduction payback if they test positive.

The basic point is this: American culture does not allow for serious discussion of the structural causes of poverty. Even among those who consider themselves liberals, by and large, the solution to poverty is psychotherapy or psychotherapeutic explanations. Some of the less inspired social work textbooks, for instance, give lip service to institutional explanations for poverty, but ultimately the solutions for poverty discussed in these books are individually based (e.g., Suppes and Wells 2003). It does seem to be the case that social workers, far from being the "bleeding heart liberals," dangerous to the social order as we so often have been painted, do little more than enforce the status quo. Certainly a few brave social workers challenge the economic system directly (such as the nationally prominent poverty researcher Mark Rank, discussed further on), but, for the most part, social workers aspire to the middle class and thus are willing to reinforce rather than transform our profoundly unjust economic system. Instead of demanding candidates with new ideas and clear plans for tax increases on the rich, we get the Casey Foundation giving money to services providers—to social workers and others who operate on fixing the poor rather than fixing our system (Tice 2003).

Indeed, most antipoverty programs are aimed at individual poor people rather than at altering our profoundly (and really, just recently) unjust taxation system (Krugman 2007: 157). Until Reagan took office, for instance, the maximum possible tax rate on income was generally 70% (145) (though it soared as high as 91% during the height of the cold war [47]). The very thought of suggesting that taxes be raised now, in the early twenty-first century, appears to verge on heresy, even though the effective tax rate on the wealthy—the actual percentage of taxes they actually pay on income—is dwarfed by the effective tax rate of an average American. Our tax system is not progressive. When the rich pay 1% of their wealth, regardless of how many actual dollars that translates to, and the lower middle class pay 16% (as any examination of the tax returns of, say, Herbert Kohl and Russ Feingold, both senators from Wisconsin, will show), we have a system that is unjust and out of whack. Even the very poor, unless they qualify for the Earned Income Tax Credit (which, granted, many do), pay a higher percentage of their incomes in taxes than do the middle class or, especially, the wealthy. Such a situation is profoundly shocking.

And the many people argues that they pay too many taxes—indeed, the wealthy will often trot a statistic like 1% of the population pays 35% of the taxes. But that's a misleading statistic: 1% of the population is wealthier than God. Of *course* they're going to pay more dollars into the pot than the rest of us. That doesn't tell us what proportion of their income in comparison to an average worker's proportion that gets paid into taxes. The highest tax bracket available on income is roughly 28% on income for federal taxes. In comparison to many European (read: developed) countries, this is very, very low. And yet the inequality between the very wealthy and the rest of us, particularly the poor, is huge, bigger than in just about any other western country. That seems supremely immoral, particularly given that the wealth of most of the wealthy folks is inherited rather than earned, and that it was built on the backs of amazingly exploited workers. Sometimes an alternative tax structure is considered—for instance, some politicians argue that a national sales tax, a consumption tax, would be equitable. It would not be. A tax on consumption will hit the poor far harder than a tax on income. It is a recipe for even further unfairness. The poor pay a higher proportion of their entire incomes, such as they are, in taxes than the middle class or the wealthy, given that they spend down just about everything they have. This suggestion is massively unjust.

In addition, there seems to be a sense in this country that we are entitled to keep all kinds of money that we earn, and that we and not that evil entity, the United States government, should decide how to spend our wages or other kinds of income. The notion is that somehow "we" are sacrificing "our" money to pay for "their" luxuries—food stamps, welfare, Section 8 housing, and so forth, I guess. There is a true sense of resentment among the middle and upper classes in this country that they have no obligation to pay taxes, that paying taxes is somehow an immoral activity, and that only suckers pay taxes. Certainly we do not want to go back to medieval times with demands for tithing and providing the aristocracy with pretty much all of the fruits of our labor, leaving only a little extra left over for us after the rich take everything. But it seems we have gone too far to the other extreme: many Americans argue that they should not have to pay anything more than minimal taxes (despite the fact that American tax rates are lower than almost any other developed country's).

The people who are financially doing relatively well, or very well, for that matter, and who are complaining about taxes do not realize how many breaks they are getting. The break, for instance, for mortgage interest amounts to an earned income tax credit for homeowners. The aim, of course, is to encourage home ownership; fair enough. But it is a grant for absolutely nothing. Everyone's tax dollars pay for a number of items we consider essential—garbage collection in some areas, hospital and other sorts of sanitary inspections, our schools, the police, the courts, emergency services like firefighters and police officers and the National Guard, postal delivery six days a week, the health department, local, state, and federal roads, sewers, an (alleged) food and environmental protection function, air traffic controllers, lighting, funds for paying to keep our parents independent instead of living with us, unemployment insurance, worker's compensation, and so many other benefits from pooling funds to build a safe and well-functioning society. Complaining about tax burdens when you are doing better than the majority of folks in this country is disingenuous at the very least, especially when you consider everything you get for what you put in. The attack on taxes by the right denies what is called by some analysts "middle-class welfare" and instead gets reconfigured as "class warfare"—as though pointing out class advantages and disadvantages is somehow a bad thing. The poor are ignored in this discussion.

"It's hardly Dickensian"

However, it could be—and often is—argued by various analysts that the United States treats its poor well if we consider "real" poverty. At least the poor are able to own (for example) a car—a used car, granted, but a car. What the apologists for the miserly American welfare state miss is that, in fact, the used car, if owned by a poor person at all, is one that will likely break down, use more gas (and thus be more expensive) than a newer car, and in general will be unreliable and more expensive to maintain than cars available to the middle class and the wealthy. We are told as well that no one in America dies from poverty; I only point out the numerous deaths of homeless men and women in American winters, the thousands of people murdered every year, and the slow (and occasional fast) deaths of millions from lack of adequate health care. Instead of focusing on the structural inequality built into the American system of penury, we are provided distracting examples of Poor People I Know who own fifty-two-inch plasma televisions or, famously, Cadillacs (Secombe 1999).

What we are talking about here is the distinction made by sociologists, economists, and others between relative poverty and absolute poverty. Absolute poverty is a measure of the most desperate poverty one can imagine: you are poor, in absolute terms, if you do not have access to clean running water, or a home, minimally defined, or a minimal amount of food for the day, or enough fuel and/or clothing to stay warm in your environment. Relative poverty, on the other hand, measures deprivation within the context of a particular society. When we look across all members of the society, those who do not have what most members of the society have would be considered poor in relative terms. In comparison to the poor in, say, Calcutta, some analysts argue, the poor in America have it made. Ask the poor of the United States if they'd trade places with a poor person in Calcutta, and guess what the answer will be. Ha! Gotcha there, says my imaginary interlocutor.

Indeed, the Heritage Foundation argues that America's poor are in fabulous shape. Apparently the poor should just stop yammering and get to work. According to Robert Rector (2007), the poor are poor because they don't work enough, they are not married, or if illegal immigrants, few valuable skills to market. The arrogance of Rector's prose is matched only by his hubris in (for instance) comparing poor children to World War I soldiers. Additionally, in Rector's view (which is representative of the conservative view), the poor aren't really poor. They're not starving, by and large. They are fat (so clearly they are "overnourished!") and clearly don't need more food than they're already getting (which only begs the question of why food banks are reporting record numbers of people in need). They have spacious (in comparison to the average European) places to live, mostly. They have televisions! And answering machines! And more square footage in which to live than most Europeans! What on earth could the poor, and those of us concerned with social justice, be complaining about! The poor have it great in the United States! Why do we leftists keep arguing that poverty is systemic? After all, Rector very clearly says, the poor live in places that "are a far cry from Dickensian squalor" (Rector 2007). Clearly the message we are to take away from Rector and the Heritage Foundation is that the poor ought to feel privileged to be poor in the United States. Life is very hard everywhere else but not for the poor in the United States.

But that isn't the point. It may be more instructive to ask a poor person (as Krugman has suggested a number of times) in the United States if she would trade places with a poor person in France, or Germany, or Sweden, or Norway, or even England or Ireland—not an average person but a poor person. When we compare social welfare benefits in European countries to our own, despite our great wealth America's minimal welfare state is an embarrassment at best. And this is not a new idea. Many scholars of the issue of American poverty, including Heilbroner, Rank, Shipler, Ehrenreich, Secombe, Katz, Jansson, and Krugman, would agree that the American welfare system is at best insulting and at worst profoundly immoral and unjust.

This is largely because it, again, is based on an assessment of the problem that revolves around individual responsibility. Instead of acknowledging our mutual obligations to each other, American culture seems to demand that we heed only one responsibility: that to ourselves. This is, actually, a profoundly un-American selfishness, as Bellah et al. (1985, 1988, 1992) point out in their various opera, and seems to have emerged, in its fullest narcissistic sense, after World War II. While a strong strain of miserliness and an attitude exemplified by "don't tread on me" has a long history in the United States, only recently have Americans been so thoroughly unwilling to act for the common good or to even recognize that such a thing might exist.

This is intimately tied to our increasing reliance on psychotherapy as explanatory for everything. By insisting that what the poor need is fiscal education, or psychotherapy to help them work out why they're so bad with money, or job training, we continue to perpetuate the problem. While certainly there are rotten poor people out there—just as there are rotten middle-class folks, and rotten rich folks—by and large what poor people need is simple: they need money. Why is that so hard to understand? What is it in our culture that simply will not grasp that fact?

In part, because, as is well established in the literature, poverty in America is seen as a moral, individual failing and not a systemic one, responsibility for poverty is moved from you, and *you*, and *you*, and me, and it is placed squarely on the lonely shoulders of the poor. We have at best a weak sense of our obligations to other people. Unlike most other human societies, our highly psychologized, psychotherapy-oriented constructions forbid us from taking on our responsibilities for our fellow citizens. We are exhorted to take responsibility for ourselves, of course (unless, as noted in chapter 2, we don't feel like it that day—something only the middle class or the wealthy can do, by the way. Refusing to do something demanded by authorities has disastrous consequences for the poor). But our sense of obligation to our fellow Americans seems to be shallow at best.

While we can see examples of this across American culture—Robert Putnam's *Bowling Alone* (2000) comes to mind—it is shown perhaps most cruelly with the poor. Indeed, it is clear that the recent crisis in the subprime lending "industry" seems to be affecting the poor and the working poor the most seriously. Now, it could be (and has been) argued that those who signed mortgage papers with subprime lenders should have, somehow, known better, perhaps bringing the questionable mortgage papers to a lawyer for examination. In point of fact, however, the subprime lenders should never have been allowed to operate in the ways that they did—using, it seems now, deceptive business practices, lying to clients and falsifying loan documents, and waving low rates in front of desperate people, assuring them that they would be able to refinance before the higher interest rates kicked in. We as Americans have failed our fellow citizens by allowing such business practices to take place. Caveat emptor should not lead to homelessness. Our government, these lenders, and we as Americans have behaved shamefully.

In many societies, such dishonest business practices could lead to far more serious consequences than, it appears, Countrywide, GMAC Finance, and Citicorp will suffer. In many societies, those operating so callously would be called out for such dangerous social transgressions, perhaps being accused of witchery or sorcery. The consequences, in many societies across the world, of a witchcraft accusation are grave, sometimes literally. You can be killed if you are a proven witch; you can be ostracized; your things can be taken from you; your children can be given to others; your wives can be redistributed; you can be beaten. Witchcraft accusations, in otherwise relatively equal societies, serve as important leveling mechanisms. They are interesting object lessons as well.

The exploitation of the poor

In our society, though, our supposedly "rational" society (the one that still thinks evolution is a silly story), those who exploit the poor often are lauded and, at worst, subject to frowny faces by Congresspeople at Important Investigative Hearings. In the current cultural climate, particularly with the Bush administration still in charge, the poor will remain exploited; the working class will suffer. Because as a culture we tend to believe that the poor are poor because they are suckers, or morally inferior, or, perhaps, genetically flawed, the poor will continue to be viewed as lacking in character, in integrity, in impulse control, when in reality what they are lacking is money.

As Shipler so poignantly illustrates in his portrait of the working poor in twenty-first-century America (Shipler 2004), while some of the poor and the working poor have made bad choices, others simply struggle to get by with dignity. For instance, Shipler notes that those who work with the poor—especially those who were themselves once poor—make judgments about some financial choices poor people make to rival assessments by Ebenezer Scrooge. Shipler discusses a group of workers who criticize their clients for having call waiting and cable (28). But, as Shipler points outs, cable in particular, even if it is $90 a month, is perhaps one of the only entertainment outlets available to the poor; additionally, Shipler says, "There are worse ways than television to escape, and why should the poor not share in the vast common ground created by American TV?" (ibid.). Apparently the poor, according to those who, presumably, wish to help them, should sit around analyzing their debt load and castigating themselves—after coming home from their second or third job. The poor, because of their presumed moral deficiencies, apparently may not ever be entertained. While they are meant to aspire to the middle class, they may not actually preemptively enter the middle class by renting a television set at usurious rates.

Once again, we see the helpers, the counselors, the social workers and psychotherapists, lambasting the poor for their deficits. What Americans don't seem to understand is just how fragile even working poverty is, and how quickly a person can slide into abject penuriousness. Shipler describes the cycle well in discussing the morass of a high-interest-rate credit card:

> On the surface, it seems odd that an interest rate can be determined by the condition of an apartment, which in turn can generate illness and medical bills, which may then translate into a poor credit rating, which limits the quality of an automobile that can be purchased, which jeopardizes a worker's reliability in getting to work, which limits promotions and restricts the wage, which confines a family to the dilapidated apartment. Such are the interlocking deficits of poverty, one reinforcing the other until an entire structure of want has been built. (Shipler 2004: 26)

So, Shipler is saying, correctly, there is a cycle of poverty, all right—but it is not intergenerationally transmitted by welfare queens who own Cadillacs. It is one that is created and sustained, by and large, through a culture of callousness and psychologized individualism, one that says that we are all responsible for our life conditions.

Usury and "short-term" loans

The poor are targeted for exploitation in ways beyond high-rate credit cards. Payday loans and car title loans constitute further ways for the poor to become mired in high-interest loans. These are loans that, it appears, are almost impossible to pay off. Some payday loan operations are noted as demanding an annual percentage rate (APR) of over 400%...400%. How on earth can any kind of reasonable society agree that these kinds of loans are a good idea? Again, the voices of the conservatives ring out: the poor shouldn't take out loans they cannot afford or do not understand. But why is it that the individual poor person is responsible for poor judgment and the banking industry is not responsible for offering immoral products?

Few poor or working poor people take out payday or car title loans to blow it on the track (though, probably, some do). No, they're paying rent, or medical bills, or a late utility bill, or, lately, to keep the car filled with gas (i.e., at this writing, approaching $4 a gallon) so they can get to Wal-Mart and their second low-wage job. Payday and car title loans are taken out by desperate people. There is, quite simply, no other option available to the poor. They have no resources. They do not have relatives with good credit or extra money, by and large, given the fact that class position in the United States, at least if you are poor, is somewhat stable. If you are poor, it's most likely that your relatives are as well. What option do you have in a society that blames you for your poverty? What option do you have in a society that refuses to recognize its responsibility to care for all members of the society? What option do you have when you are told that you, and solely you, are responsible for the conditions in which you live? No option, really. You have no option other than usury and exploitation and being blamed for all of your ills.

Your sickness belongs to you

However, how is it possible that a child is responsible for his contracting of HIV? How is it possible that a child is responsible for her cleft palate? How could it possibly be, in any rational world, that a just society deprives children of needed health care? How could it possibly be, in any sane universe, that parents must be bankrupted before their fellow citizens, through the help of the federal government (more specifically SCHIPS, or State Children's Health Insurance Program), will give them a hand in dealing with medical conditions that are curable? If we as a society are going to make decisions about parceling out health care, why are the poor and the dispossessed the last to receive adequate care? Why do the children of middle class and the wealthy deserve good medical treatment while the children of the poor and the working poor are relegated to the trash bin?

We do not want to see the poor's suffering. We simply don't believe that someone who is working cannot get medical care, and, I guess, we believe that Medicaid is some kind of luxury item. We just cannot—will not—comprehend such desperation in this wealthy nation. Our culture tells us that, if you want it bad enough, you can succeed—including, apparently, those wonderful aspirations to actually get to a private doctor's waiting room.

Just recently, in 2007, George W. Bush vetoed various versions of SCHIPS. He objected to Americans paying for the health care of other Americans. Echoing the beliefs of at least some U.S. citizens (though, it must be noted, the country pretty much has veered to the left of Bush's reactionary positions as of this writing), Bush rejected SCHIPS because it would supplant private insurance (Lee 2007: A03)—apparently a bad thing. Though Bush's position is relatively far to the right of most of the country, the country apparently did find itself uncomfortable with the notion that some middle-class families would be eligible for this benefit (since the vetoes have not been overridden). Once again, the idea that citizens ought to help out other citizens is nowhere to be found in this discussion. Once again, the idea that we owe each anything at all is absent. Instead, we are all supposed to stand on our own two feet (assuming we have both of them, something that cannot be assumed so blithely) and look after our own.

The others who work

And heaven forbid that we even dare to suggest that undocumented workers might deserve a small piece of the pie. Of course, since we won't provide minimal funding for the poor who are actual citizens in this country—though the level of disenfranchisement seems to be growing through laws like those in Indiana (upheld recently by the Supreme Court) requiring relatively expensive forms of identification before being able to vote—why on earth would we take care of those who are not citizens? We continue to hear incredibly hateful speech about undocumented workers—the workers who provide the lion's share of labor to harvest and produce our food—and rarely do we see any acknowledgement of the great sacrifices and tremendous hardships of those workers. No, instead, we get states attempting (unsuccessfully) to insist that they have a right to pass English-only laws, so that immigrants—legal and illegal—may not vote in their native languages, may not be counseled in their native languages, may not be instructed in their native languages...the list of xenophobic and ethnocentric outrages can go on and on.

Undocumented workers are among the poorest of the poor, and they have the fewest protections. Even if we allowed for a legitimate discussion of relative and absolute poverty, just a cursory glance at how undocumented workers live in most parts of the country would reveal shocking conditions of absolute poverty. In Florida, undocumented workers are regularly sprayed with pesticides by cropdusters and suffer from a variety of both culture-bound and environmentally caused illnesses. This is, of course, in addition to their significant underpayment; minimum wages do not apply to those illegally in the country (so that Burger King continues to refuse to provide a 2 cent per bucket raise in pay to Florida tomato pickers; McDonald's has done so). Indeed, the Urban Institute estimates that most undocumented workers are routinely paid far less than American citizens: "About two-thirds of undocumented workers earn less than twice the minimum wage, compared with only one-third of all workers" (Passel et al. 2004). In other words, the undocumented poor are exploited even more than the poor who are American citizens.

Now, the conservative pundits, such as The Heritage Foundation, will argue that undocumented workers are to blame for their poverty (as noted, The Heritage Foundation apparently thinks that the poor in the United States aren't really very poor at all; Rector 2007). According to Robert Rector, undocumented workers (or "illegal immigrants," as he calls this group) are poor because their behavior causes them to be poor. They are uneducated and they have children out of wedlock (Rector 2007). Apparently the fact that they are paid significantly less than American citizens has nothing to do with their poverty.

The problem, of course, is that those of us who are (temporarily) more fortunate owe a great debt to the poor and the working poor. It is the poor and the working poor who labor for inhumanely low wages, a minimum wage that, despite being raised, still is not enough to bring a person over the poverty line. By refusing to provide living wages, employers garner great dividends for their shareholders but forget the rest of us—the stakeholders in this country. In other words, poverty is not the result of profoundly immoral and psychologically deficient behavior on the part of the poor. It is the result of exploitation by the rich. But that analysis is always and evermore rejected—of course it is. To accept a structural explanation for a shameful condition, something that should not occur in a nation as wealthy and fortunate as ours, would mean that the rich would have to give up some of their privileges so that a just society could be had.

So, instead, the poor get financial management classes, and GEDs, and job training, and psychotherapy, and anger management, and jail. Their children are taught to aspire for more (Kusserow 2004) but are not provided with the minimum of tools required to build that white picket fence. Children in general are profoundly psychologized as well; it is to that population I turn next.

Chapter 4

The Kids Aren't All Right

In 1996, two teenaged boys took assault weapons to school and massacred twelve students and one teacher before turning the weapons on themselves. In all, fifteen people died at Columbine High School. Despite the fact that school violence, largely perpetrated by African Americans and Latinos, had been skyrocketing in the 1980s and many more people died, no one paid any attention to the problem until European American children began dying. That in itself is appalling. The explanations invoked, however, to discuss the frightening new phenomenon were even worse. The Columbine murderers were discovered to be mentally ill, or so the media declared.

Parents and families have nothing to do with juvenile violence, apparently, and neither does the larger culture. At least, that's what was clear from media discussions with "experts." Any explorations of America's violent culture, for instance, as contributing to the actions of teenagers (or younger children, for that matter) were seen as unacceptable attempts to help children "evade responsibility" for their actions. If someone tried to say that the Columbine parents—who seemingly knew, and certainly should have known, that their boys had weapons, explosives, and the like—failed in their child-rearing efforts, psychologists rushed in to tell the world that the parents had suffered enough.

Such positions are completely irresponsible. In addition, they are wrong. The Columbine parents are at fault here. The larger culture is at fault here. It is most likely that the two boys, left to their own devices as they were, were not mentally ill but responding in an understandable if unforgivable way to American cultural messages about manhood, emotion, violence, and weapons. They provide us with important ways to analyze the treatment of teenagers in American society and to contemplate its effects on the future of the democratic process in the United States.

The Columbine tragedy has been sadly repeated in more recent history. Cho Seung-Hui, a twenty-three-year-old legal resident of the United States, originally from Korea, deliberately murdered thirty-two people at Virginia Tech in Blacksburg, Virginia in April

2007. News reports consistently refer to him as a "psychopath" (*Economist* 2007), "violent and erratic" (*The Seattle Times*—Apuzzo 2007), and, of course, the inevitable "loner" (*The New York Times*—Hauser 2007). Now, Cho's case is a bit different, as, at twenty-three, he not only was no longer living under the direct supervision of his parents, unlike the Columbine killers, but, in fact, Cho had clear, identifiable, and serious mental illness issues, enough to hospitalize him several times.

And, of course, there is the even more recent set of shootings at Northern Illinois University (NIU), again carried out by a man in his twenties. Steven Kazmierczak was characterized as having "a troubled mind" and as a former mental patient (MSNBC February 16, 2008 serves as an example). The Virginia Tech massacre and the NIU shootings are relevant since it is clear that our concept of adolescence has extended past the teenage years. The notion of adolescence as a period of apprenticeship now seems to carry on through to about thirty years old.

What is a teenager?

The typical psychological description of teenagers invokes hormones, identity, conflicts, and emotional states. Teenagers, according to the child development experts, are beings largely at the mercy of biological processes. It is, for these experts, "natural" for adolescents to be moody, lustful, rebellious, and risk-taking, given their raging hormones. Lately they argue that it is "natural" for teenagers to sleep late, claiming to have indisputable biological proof of brain differences between teenagers and the rest of us (Ritter 2007: A1, A10). They are of course incorrect.

The peculiarly indulgent view of adolescence is an American artifact. Most teenagers across the world do not engage in the kinds of behavior we allow American children. Indeed, many teenagers across the world are involved in adult activities—marriage, child-rearing, earning a living, fighting wars. The American—and, less so, Western European—version of adolescence is one that emerges from privilege. We have been able to extend childhood to ridiculous lengths, forgiving infantile behavior far beyond biological childhood. Raging hormones do not create American adolescence. American culture does.

For instance, the killers at Columbine were believed to be very unhappy young men. According to accounts after their deaths, they felt excluded, picked on, teased, isolated, and rejected. Coupled with the psychologists' construction of adolescence as a naturally stormy time, the analysts concurred that teenagerhood plus rejection equaled murder. Although some more reasonable folks argued that many teenagers are rejected and do not, despite the storms of adolescence, murder thirteen people, most discussions of Columbine centered on the reading of this incident as an understandable, if appallingly exaggerated, result of adolescence. The exaggeration was the undiagnosed mental illnesses from which both boys allegedly suffered (though, in fairness, it must be pointed out that at least one of the young men had been marked out as Attention Deficit-Hyperactivity Disorder (ADHD)—technically a mental illness but not the kind being discussed by the experts). In addition, the boys' search for "identity" led them down dangerous paths of "Goth culture" apparently under the unseeing eyes of their parents. Furthermore, one of the boys had moved often, frequently being the "new kid" in school. All of these factors, according to the experts, led to the boys' murderous and suicidal rampage.

Similarly, the Virginia Tech murderer, Cho, has been characterized in ridiculous and typically American ways. Irrationality reigns: there are legislators talking about arming the professors, or people blaming Asians for killings, or professors for not knowing how to read minds. The same thing happened after 9/11 and Katrina: why did these things happen? Well, according to some, it's because we're not holy enough, as the late Jerry Falwell and Pat Robertson claimed after both 9/11 and the devastation of Hurricane Katrina.

Humans, in our great hubris, assume or, better, demand that there are reasonable explanations for unreasonable events, and that those explanations are available to us through our anthropomorphic supernatural beings. Many humans simply can't tolerate the explanation: tragedy happens, and it happens often enough to make it regular if not predictable. This apparent need for a deterministic universe, one in which nothing happens by chance, seems to comfort people, despite it being about as accurate as a ten-day weather forecast.

We are never going to know the mind of the shooter. Psychological autopsies are worth precisely nothing, since there is no one available to refute them. Profilers cannot predict a thing. It's all smoke and mirrors, masquerading as "science." Life is tragic. "Why?" is pointless. It is. It happened. This series of deaths was horrific. If guns had not been available, this would not have happened on this scale. Period. What's more important is not "why" but "how." And, without diminishing the very real suffering of thousands, if not millions, of people, we need to remember that hundreds of thousands of people have died in Iraq since 9/11. What for? The point is not to make a cheap political statement but to note that, for so many of our fellow Earth inhabitants, random useless death is a constant event, not a horrifying and unusual tragedy. It's not to say that we may not mourn Virginia Tech; it's not to say that we should not problem solve in attempts to prevent future massacres. However, we should acknowledge that the bulk of human experience has involved the accidently and randomly tragic; life, daily existence, for many people across the world, includes daily death.

I saw an excerpt of Cho's video despite my best attempts to avoid it. My first thought was, quite frankly, "you are a big baby. Get over yourself." He may have acted very badly (well, obviously; I mean before the shootings) and have been "depressed." He appeared to me to be a self-righteous, overgrown idiot who compensated for a lack of competence socially and intellectually by going all gangsta. I am not making light of this young man and his horrible behaviors. The video indicates to me, however, someone who paid far too much attention to his interiority. Creative writing may not have been the best outlet for him.

Nowhere is culture mentioned in any of this, except as a rejected throwaway line. It cannot be denied that American culture is a highly violent one; when coupled with the overweening sense, promoted by the cultural dominance of psychotherapeutic values, of a person's emotional self-importance, Columbine begins to look like a microcosm of American hyperindividualism. The Columbine murderers, and the Virginia Tech and NIU young men as well, felt rejected and isolated. They understood, most likely, that it is impermissible to feel rejected and isolated. They should instead be feeling happy and accepted. In their infantile attention to how they felt, the Columbine murderers decided to use that good old American initiative and do something about their feelings—removing the apparent source of their pain.

Although certainly they could have made other choices, the Columbine murderers were acting on a dominant cultural script. If you are miserable, it is up to you to change the situation making you miserable. No other explanation is possible. Furthermore, your feelings are your feelings and are neutral if not wonderful. It is very likely that the parents of the Columbine murderers, engaged as they probably were in enacting American dominant cultural child-rearing practices, encouraged the boys to attend to their feelings to the exclusion of changing behavior or intellectual processes.

Baby boomer parents—and certainly the parents of the Columbine murderers are baby Boomers—spend much time helping their children explore their feelings. One possible result of such an indulgent and unrealistic child-rearing method is the production of children who believe that they are the center of the universe and whose feelings must always be heeded and respected.

Juvenile justice and ethnicity

This seems to be true regardless of ethnicity for the most part. While we know that children of color are disproportionately arrested, tried, and sentenced in comparison to their European American counterparts (as is true for their elders), the feelings of adolescents are accepted as valid by most participants in the juvenile justice system. The results of this acceptance of course vary by ethnicity and class: middle-class European American children receive therapy while children of color receive punishment. But emotional responses remain important regardless of ethnicity despite the prejudicial nature of the juvenile justice system.

Whether placed in overtly therapeutic or clearly punitive settings, convicted juvenile offenders receive psychotherapy. It is believed, apparently, that therapy can help. In particular, children who commit violent crimes are provided with "anger management" (as are men who are repeat domestic violence offenders). Anger management is useless, of course. It does not work (Lewin 2001: 2). Even its proponents cannot offer any clear evidence of its efficacy—yet it continues to be promoted as a cure-all for a violent American culture. It is a typically American solution for an American problem—we treat the individual without changing the culture. So juvenile offenders are required to submit to anger management classes; they are required to accept full responsibility for their inabilities to control themselves. Parents who promoted the lack of control to which young people are now subject have no responsibility in this scenario. Parents are hapless victims of their children, only meaning well by encouraging children to continually take their emotional pulses.

The problem is the "diagnosis"

The trouble with children today seems to be their interiority—or so our culture tells us. If a person is on the political Right, she likely will say that the interiority is flawed, perhaps due to a turning away from God or "family values," lack of discipline, or genetic inferiority; fixing the interiority requires tough, if not brutal, love—juvenile boot camps, adult jurisprudence for what are seen as adult crimes, if even committed by children. On the other hand, if a person is on the political Left, he will argue that a child's difficult interiority is due perhaps to undiagnosed ADHD, personality disorder, depression (that's a favorite on the Left), or bipolar disorder; such emotional difficulty requires psychotherapy if it's to be repaired—anger management, group therapy, self-esteem building, medication to be sure. On the Right, solutions to today's "troubled youth" are punitive while on the left they are therapeutic—but they both see the individual child as the locus of both the problem and the solution. Where is culture in all of this? Nowhere.

Yet our child-rearing methods have produced the behavior about which we are concerned. The American child-rearing focus on independent individualism and a concomitant emphasis on authentic emotional expression, even for infants, help to produce children who rather unsteadily stand on their own two feet while attempting to identify their feelings so that their parents can validate those emotions. By encouraging authentic emotional expression of independent individuals, we wind up with infantile, self-absorbed people who concentrate more on their own feelings and desires than larger thoughts and ideas. By denying that children's emotions may be, well, childish, in need of direction and guidance, requiring some instruction on actually suppressing some emotions that are socially harmful—greed, for instance, or envy, or selfishness—we produce children who feel completely free to express themselves emotionally all the time. We produce children have no sense of standards, or rigor, or self-discipline. We produce children who believe they are entitled to just about anything they want, right away, because they feel like having it. And in this culture of luxury, of privilege, in the United States, many parents go deep into hock in order to obtain extra televisions and computers and brand-new cars for teenagers to keep their kids happy (see, e.g., Quart's 2003 discussion of $50,000 bar mitzvahs).

Most parents in the United States either agree with the child-rearing methods discussed in the popular media or by "experts," or they have to pretend to agree unless they wish to risk losing their kids to child welfare agencies. Parents who are less than friendly with their children are violating some serious child-rearing norms established by Baby Boomers, based on supposedly scientific evidence.

Pediatricians, for instance, seem to think that they actually know something about child development (which, quite frankly, they don't) and that children need this, that, or the other thing. Children don't "need," for instance, to be independent. Americans need for them to be so. There is absolutely no evidence cross-culturally that this is a universal human need; it is an American creation. There is no evidence that children "need" to be friendly with parents; it's just the way we do it here. Children are rather hardy beings, not fragile souls. Only in a country where children so rarely die could we be so very sentimental about our kids.

There is a clear connection between the Entitlement Children who live in what I've lately been calling the Barney World of Equality, the parents who raise them (and who have more debt, but a better "lifestyle," than any generation that preceded them), road rage, increased violence, alleged increases in ADHD (what we're seeing, I think, is not more ADHD but far many more expectations of children), and, in short, an incredibly indulgent society. We grown-ups often indulge ourselves (why else are there McMansions or Hummers?) and we indulge our little sugarpies, so much so that the little darlings appear to be in charge of the adults.

That is the most frightening aspect of all of this. Children should not be given choices, as they are children and don't know anything. But pediatricians, while well meaning, have so little understanding of what children need biologically and how to separate that from what is culturally bound. Children do not need their own rooms; they do not need autonomy; their opinions do not need to be taken seriously. Again, that's just how we do it. We put their lousy, messy paintings proudly on the fridge (or, worse, frame it and call it art). We think that their opinions on War are legitimate. Apparently they need their own televisions and computers. We appear to be terrified of the short people. This is very bad.

However, as Robert Bly (1996) pointed out in *The Sibling Society* (and Neil Postman [1994] made similar remarks in *The Disappearance of Childhood*), there seem to be no adults any longer. There are just teenagers and wannabe teenagers. It's worrisome when students or parents talk about each other as "friends." Certainly parents, in our culture, are friendly with children. I really, really hope, though, that parents are not treating their children as friends, a reciprocal relationship that undermines parenting. Parents can be their children's friends; children cannot be their parents' friends, though, at least not until adulthood (and even then it's fraught with difficulty!).

The idea of "choices" belongs to a wealthy nation such as the United States. Choices like "would you prefer peas or carrots" are completely unavailable to many people in the world, including most children. Having choices is a luxury; from an evolutionary standpoint, choices are not necessary for a child's basic development. They are, however, a clear part of American culture and certainly children in the United States must be shown how to handle them. Still, though, the option for choices changes, and patience with young people ebbs as they finish high school.

What a shock it must be for young people when they get to college or the workplace and discover that their needs and choices in fact do not come first. If they are lucky, professors will judge them mightily when in college; their bosses are not going to be all that interested in their employees' reasons for being late ("I broke up with my boyfriend and I'm depressed"). If young people raised in the current American child-rearing climate are unlucky, so shall we older folks be. We will not be taken care of by our children when we get older, because they won't feel like it. American productivity will be completely lost. Many young people couldn't care less, for instance, about either the future of Social Security or the injustice of the American economic system, as long as neither one has anything to do with them. What we have here is a generation of infantile, narcissistic children who refuse to look outside of themselves and their needs, focusing almost exclusively on their feelings and their desires. What we have here are a bunch of babies—and we raised them (or not, as the case may be).

We know very well by now that women and men of the Boomer generation overwhelmingly are two-job (or more) families. Few parents stay home with children any longer. There seems to be no questioning the truism that getting along in today's world takes more than one income. But why is that? Why is the Boomer generation unable to save money (the latest reports indicate that on average the United States has a negative savings rate of –2% per month—in other words, we spend more than we have and don't save at all)? As part of the infantilism that permeates American culture, my generation seems unable to deny their impulses as adults. How can we expect them to deny their children's desires? Many of my students, for instance, grew up a) in their own bedrooms that b) were completely outfitted electronically—with fancy stereos, computers, and televisions. Few of them had to work for those items, or wait, perhaps a long time, to obtain a DVD player. Their parents simply provided such things to their children. Long gone, it appears, are the days when fighting over what television program to watch was a favorite activity of siblings. These days, brothers and sisters, if there even are any siblings, have their own televisions.

Young people are suffering as a result. Self-assertion rather than patience seems to be the value; multitasking instead of concentration has become important. A constant murmuring in the background—of the television, and, probably, the CD player and downloaded music from the computer—accompanies young people's activities. Young people—and, let's face it, Baby Boomers as well—cannot face silence. It is torture to them, it appears—and therein lies the suffering. Children who are unable to concentrate are not taught to do so. Instead, they are "diagnosed" with ADHD and drugged with Ritalin. Indeed, Boomers are beginning to believe that they too are adult victims of ADHD and require drugs as well.

Drugging children to keep them quiet instead of removing the stimuli and teaching self-discipline is a poor child-rearing strategy, but it is the one promoted by the psychotherapeutic metaphor in dominant American culture. The emerging discussion of ADHD is that, somehow, it involves chemical interactions in the brain (though there is no physiological test for ADHD, only behavioral markers), and Ritalin or Clonidine, stimulants that somehow alter that brain chemistry in a child diagnosed as ADHD, are the only solution. While occasionally lip service is paid to classroom size or chronic electronic overstimulation in our culture or the hurried, overscheduled "lifestyle" of today's youth (from school to soccer to—gasp—two to three hours of homework a night), the problem is seen as fundamentally and intrinsically individual in nature, and the solution is individual in nature. Occasionally a family will decide to cut out some activities, but for the most part medical management is most important. This is, of course, odd, since Boomers grew up in classrooms of forty to fifty children, yet somehow managed, for the most part, to learn how to concentrate and be responsible without medication. (Sometimes the rejoinder to such a remark is that there was plenty of ADHD around but it just wasn't diagnosed. That may have been all for the better.)

So what we have is a growing population of children diagnosed as defective and requiring chemical correction. At present, approximately 7.8% of all children have been identified as exhibiting ADHD (Centers for Disease Control 2005), and boys are diagnosed at nearly three times the rate as girls. Interestingly, far more African American girls than girls of other ethnicities are slapped with an ADHD label, particularly in junior high school (Reid et al.

1998: 187). Assertive young women who face a constant barrage of sexuality, drug use, and poverty (and assertiveness could well be a terrific and positive response to a racist, sexist environment) are viewed by dominant American culture, as enacted by teachers, school administrators, and medical personnel, as ill, requiring calming down through psychopharmacology. Is this really the best way to rear children?

Interestingly, in one of the only truly cross-cultural studies of ADHD, anthropology Ken Jacobson has found that English children—genetically and biologically very similar to European American children—are far less likely to be diagnosed with ADHD (and therefore are far less likely to take Ritalin) than are American children and especially boys. Less than 1% of English schoolchildren are seen as hyperactive (Zuckerman 2000). British schoolteachers, physicians, and psychiatrists read behaviors used to diagnose American hyperactivity as normal childish behavior; in fact, Jacobson could see no objective difference between the behavior of "normal" English kids and the very few diagnosed as ADHD (ibid.). This outlook seems as, if not more, effective for English children than Ritalin is for American children (ibid.). If ADHD is biologically based, one would conclude that behavioral, cultural, and systemic explanations would be ineffective; the same behaviors would be noted, particularly in cultures so similar as America and Britain. However, if we draw the conclusions apparently being drawn by the English and Jacobson, that ADHD is a cultural and systemic problem, not a biological one, than the increasing use of biological and psychopharmaceutical solutions—psychotropic drugs—has cultural and not physiological dynamics. In other words, ADHD can be included in what psychological anthropologists call culture-bound syndromes—created and maintained by dominant cultural systems of meaning (see chapter 5 for a further discussion).

What this means that an exploration of ADHD, and even more critically, autism, from a cultural viewpoint is crucial. Why is it that more and more American children are being viewed as troublesome, as mentally ill? And a perception of mental illness on the part of America's youth is indeed what's going on. Is it only that parents these days have scant time for the children, as alluded to before? Is the sense that American children are out of control due to a burgeoning and newly dawning sense that mental illness is far more common than thought? Or is it our dominant culture?

It is, by and large, American dominant culture. Our child-rearing methods have begun to produce incredibly rude and self-centered children. ADHD and the resultant Ritalin prescriptions, in this view, can be seen as the resignation of parents from their jobs as child-rearers. Rather than squelching bad behavior and teaching self-discipline, rather than punishing self-absorption and rewarding common courtesy, parents have thrown up their hands and passed off responsibility for their children's behavior to experts.

But it isn't just the parents' fault. The dominant American culture and its adherents, and, if we are to believe Bill Epstein, the American electorate as a whole, has decided that medical solutions—individual, psychological explanations—are more "socially efficacious" (to use Epstein's [1997, 2002] term) than getting at the root of the problem. Social policy regarding American children seems to put our kids into two groups: the victims (and, of course, there are far too many of them) and the monsters. Victims almost exclusively are medicated and therapized. Monsters are medicated and locked up. Psychotropic medication is what the two groups have in common. Individualistic solutions, rather than cultural ones, are what the two groups share.

What would a cultural solution look like? How about a complete ban on marketing to children? How about a complete ban on the manufacture of video games, violent or otherwise? How about a complete ban on producing television geared toward children? How about a movement away from computer-based "learning" and a move toward pencils, papers, and books? How about the closing down of Hollywood, so that children will not ninja-turtle-kick each other to death? What if our society began actually reading again? What would happen if no guns were available to anyone, anywhere, in the United States? What if our economic system was drastically altered so that in fact all children would have the same opportunities—not the same outcomes necessarily but the same opportunities? What if all schools had the same levels of funding? What if teachers were educated in subject matter rather than classroom management and diversity and self-esteem issues? What if parents actually had time to rear their children, or, better yet, were able to live in extended family groups in which many people had a hand in children and their futures?

Few of these are realistic solutions. But the removal of agents of violence from schools, neighborhoods, and homes—guns, video games, violent movies—would be a start. Allowing parents to spend time with their children—and perhaps not worrying about paying that $200,000 mortgage, maybe even living in apartments if they can't afford a house—in fruitful, non-electronic play, discussion, and work could be helpful. A movement toward common courtesy by all of us, including children, and the abandonment of foul language from our vocabularies, all of us, can only make our children's lives, and our lives, better.

Common courtesy, however, is the enemy of psychotherapy. Common courtesy requires thinking of others before yourself and is thus seen by psychotherapy as inauthentic, unhealthy, and co-dependent. It might be all right to be courteous to strangers, but to "fake" a good mood in front of intimates is really understood to be a bad thing. Yet social life, from an evolutionary and ethnographic point of view, requires that we cover our most difficult feelings with at least a veneer of cheerfulness. That is something that we Americans have forgotten, it seems, and it is showing, and badly, in our children.

We have a fairly disordered set of child-rearing strategies, to be sure; they are leading, in my view, to perennially discontented children, always wanting more but, even worse, and more sadly, wanting to be heard, to be validated, to express themselves (even when they know so little about the world). These discontented children, our American adolescents, are frightening on so many levels. They have little sense of time and silence; they wish, it seems, to be entertained constantly (certainly they view some of their professors as television programs that are required to entertain them—it appears that sometimes they wish they had the remote so they could switch channels). Levels of concentration are nil; depth of understanding seems irrelevant to so many of them. Listening does not seem to happen; instead, there seem to be continual mutual monologues, carried on with cell phones in bathrooms or at parties when sitting next to each other (or so my students tell me). Adolescents today seem not to know where they live; they seem sure, even more than ever, that what they know is all that is worth knowing.

How can American democracy survive, tattered as it is today, with heirs who will not read, cannot write, and seem, by and large, uninterested in anyone but themselves? I do fear for our society. It is, I think, our job as anthropologists to help our society come up with alternatives in which our youth can see themselves as connected to each other in systems of meaning and thought and dreams; it is our job to deny that hope is gone and to aver that change, good change, change that connects us and demonstrates our interconnectedness, change that requires that occasionally we sacrifice for someone else, is possible and good. It is our job as professors to demand a basic literacy and numeracy. It is our job as Americans to insist, among other things, on more from our schools housing our adolescents and from our fellow citizens rearing children. And ultimately, then, it is our job, as human beings, to sympathize less and demand more from our children.

Sexual and physical abuse of children

It certainly is far too simplistic to argue that the lack of common courtesy has resulted in the rash of reports of child abuse in the last two decades and more recently in the context of the Catholic Church. Indeed, a victim of sexual or physical abuse has absolutely no moral call to be courteous; a swift quick to the nether regions of the abuser would probably be far more useful. In fact, it may be that an excess of courtesy on the part of victims, of not challenging adults, has something to do with the current sexual abuse crisis in the Catholic Church. It is absolutely so that the perpetrators of sexual abuse are exceedingly impolite (which, after all, is one way to look at criminal behavior—that is, behavior that society has decided is so completely out of bounds that it must be overtly recognized as wrong and punishable).

However, where the central analysis of this book comes in here—the overwhelming use of the psychotherapeutic metaphor in dominant American culture—is not that child abuse victims are using the metaphor but that the perpetrators are. In other words, like the children described above, perpetrators of sexual abuse do not understand themselves as having limits. Like so many Americans—though, of course, a gross exaggeration—perpetrators of sexual abuse experience an impulse for whatever reason and give into it. I say "for whatever reason" because there is absolutely no clear evidence regarding the genesis of pedophilia—arguments that it is due to physiological or genetic reasons, or Freudian reasons, or family dynamics reasons, or homosexual tendencies (given that most pedophiles are heterosexual, that one is particularly silly), or even gender and sexism reasons: all of these explanations are completely unproven.

The fact is that by continuing to search for faulty interiority on the part of pedophiles, of all pedophiles, without analyzing dominant American culture, will simply continue pedophilia (so will continued celibacy on the part of priests, but that's a different discussion). Our culture, an oddly Puritanical yet pornographic one (as discussed in chapter 1), encourages the expression of impulses.

Pedophiles experience the impulse to fondle little girls, or sodomize young men, and—rather than having the self-discipline to contain themselves—act on that impulse. It's simply more of the same. A feeling is experienced and, in our culture, it must be expressed regardless of the consequence.

This is not to condone pedophilia or forgive its perpetrators. The larger point is that those who sexually abuse do so in the context of a dominant American culture that allows—demands—authentic expression of one's self. Most of us would argue that we do not even experience the impulse to be sexual with children, and that is so, thank goodness. However, at this point, most Americans would agree that authentic emotional expression is better than false suppression, or even worse, repression, of feelings. The focus on the self, outside of context, outside of systems that may insist on proper courteous behavior, outside of anything but one's interiority, has helped to create many of the problems our children, and we, face today. We have assisted in the abuse of our children through unquestioning compliance with dominant American culture.

See Spot. Run, Spot, run!

We have collaborated as well with the growing ignorance of our children. It has been reported (Sykes 1995) that nearly 20% of high school graduates could not identify the United States on a blank world map and that half of young Americans cannot locate New York on a U.S. map (Roach 2006), much less Iraq or Afghanistan. Few young people are required to write or research term papers in high school; they seem to be reading fewer and fewer books. Some curricula instruct students to attend to the "process" of writing and not to worry about such minor things as grammar, sentence construction, and spelling (since grammatical conventions are arbitrary, presumably assembled by white guys to be used by white guys and to oppress all Others). It is acceptable—judging from the comments I receive from college students—to declare a subject "boring" and expect to be entertained.

Indeed, rather than educating children today, we seem to be keeping them stimulated through electronics (again, with the result that concentration is shot). "Television in the classroom" is not only a trademarked phrase but apparently also a good thing. Watching videos of Hamlet, rather than reading it, is an alternate pedagogical technique, not laziness on the part of the junior-high teacher.

A recent television ad for "Leapfrog" demonstrates the convenience, for parents, of an electronic book equipped with a computer-generated voice that sounds out letters for children. The ad begins with Dad driving the ubiquitous mini-van, Mom in the front seat, and the presumably only child in the back with his Leapfrog trying to read. The child stumbles over "jet" and Dad cheerfully exhorts his son to "sound it out." The boy takes the little pen and a male computer voice generates the sounds of the word in the time-honored tradition, and the little boy triumphantly repeats "j-e-t JET!" Mom and Dad beam at each other. How wonderful, they seem to be saying to each other. Our little boy can read!

The only problem is this: this mom and dad had nothing to do with it other than buying "Leapfrog" and putting it in their little boy's grubby hands. Rather than taking the time with their son, they—like so many people today—are multitasking and leaving essential instruction to the experts, both animate and inanimate. Granted, it can be very annoying and time-consuming to actually sit down day after day and night after night and teaching children important fundamentals. It's even more difficult to serve as a role-model and do some adult reading (the best predictor, by the way, of children's success at reading is that their parents are serious readers [Newman n.d.]). Children, and some adults (or so it seems), find life much more fascinating when it happens through electronic devices rather than through simple walks in the park or through sharing chapters from books or through actual discussion at the dinner table.

And heaven forbid that life might occasionally be boring. A report on the local news in the St. Louis area a few years back indicated that "cruising" in cars in a particular neighborhood was causing so much traffic backup, and, now and then, some gunfire, that paramedics were unable to penetrate the area to collect, for instance, a man with two broken legs. When interviewed, the young people driving around (in this instance, the teenagers were African American) said they cruised because "there's nothing to do around here" (KSDK-TV 2003). Given that these young people had cars—very nice cars, in some cases—they cannot say that they can't get to the library, or to the soup kitchen to feed the homeless, or to a job, or to summer school. All of those things, one must assume, would be boring.

It could well be that Postman, in *The Disappearance of Childhood* (1994), is correct. Although talking about television (the book was drafted before the spread of computers and video games to many homes), Postman argues that the electronic media have co-opted both childhood and adulthood. By pitching everything to teenagers, and, now, younger children, including sex and violence, Americans have blurred the lines that used to exist between childish and grown-up ways. Postman cites just one small example, having to do with fast-food outlets such as McDonald's and Burger King, which, he says, do not seem to discriminate between adult and childish pitches for their commodities, especially since there are more adults eating "junk food" than children:

> This is no trivial point: it seems that many have forgotten when adults were supposed to have higher standards than children in their conception of what is and is not edible. Indeed, it was a mark of movement toward adulthood when a youngster showed an inclination to reject the kind of fare that gives the junk-food industry its name. I believe we can say rather firmly that this marker of the transition to adulthood is now completely obliterated. (Postman 1994:128–129)

Adults and children are all of a piece, now. Adult tastes have moved from the sophisticated to the bland. We take our food recommendations from children.

Witness the 2003 commercial for "Old Country Buffet," a nationwide chain of steam-table, cafeteria-style "restaurants." Geared toward families, apparently (and the occasional senior citizen looking forward to the early-bird special and the AARP discount before 6 p.m.), this eatery does not serve alcohol (Old Country Buffet advertisement 2003/2004). Instead, heapin' mounds of ribs, mashed potatoes, meatloaf, soft-serve ice cream, and similar delectables pique the interests of the admittedly adorable moppets in the 2003 ad as they discuss how many napkins you'll need if you eat the ribs (for instance). "I really like it there," declares one towheaded boy. "We always go on Wednesdays."

Why is it, one has to wonder, that children dictate the dining habits of their parents? Let's think of a typical Thanksgiving dinner in a Boomer household. Though a gorgeous standing rib roast is awaiting consumption, the only child in the vicinity announces "yuck!" Rather than saying something like "I'm sorry you don't want to be a grown-up and eat grown-up food but that's all there is," the child's parent (and chef) apologizes profusely to the child and has the adults wait while the parent took twenty minutes to prepare macaroni and cheese. On Thanksgiving.

Since when are children in charge of menu selection, or anything having to do with adult activities? Well, it appears that it's been since adults have abdicated adulthood. Only thirty years ago, children dressed in one way and adults in another. That's no longer true.

Indeed, children—and I do mean children younger than ten—have available to them see-through blouses, tight-tight jeans, crop-tops, high heels, mini-skirts, and other kinds of provocative clothing that only certain kinds of adult women would once dared to have worn (to say nothing of makeup and other cosmetics).

Children seem to think that they are the equals, if not the superiors, of adults. Once again, the dominant culture's use of the psychotherapeutic metaphor reigns supreme. Since the logic of the metaphor includes the proposition that all feelings are equivalent and useful, and further that all humans have feelings, including children, that are worthy of respect and are not to be judged, it is simply a short jump to concluding that children's feelings are as equivalent and useful as the emotional life of adults and hence children are equivalent to adults. In other words, children are encouraged to explore and express their feelings as thoroughly as adults, making them equal to adults. A six-year-old child's pronouncement that "smoking is yucky" is applauded, or a nine-year-old's analysis that "war is bad" is received with solemnity—as though children know anything about either subject. Indeed, we solicit children's opinions as though they are useful dissertations on the state of the world or even the state of the dinner meal. We even get suggestions from the children themselves about how to keep them from hurting themselves and others. Parents seem unwilling to limit the behavior of their children with any regularity.

For instance, I see so many parents these days scampering after their toddlers, saying "no" to this and "leave that alone" to that. Either you have to remove the temptation from the child, or remove the child from the temptation. Whatever happened to playpens? How about cordless phones? If you keep your child confined, she will not be reaching for the phone cord or the CDs or the cat's tail. A home can never be completely childproofed, hence the frantic running around. But confined to a playpen a child is out of danger but still in sight. If you don't like a playpen, pick her up and put her on your hip. Giving a child free access to the house and then expecting the child to act like an adult is a recipe for disaster and, sadly, for abusive behavior. Many parents seem to have gigantic expectations of their children—whether it is expecting one year olds to control themselves, or seven year olds to think rationally about Halloween candy, or (insert childish behavior here). Having adult expectations of children, whether it is leaving phone cords alone or being able to talk rationally about one's feelings, is an abusive stance ultimately. Part of the phenomenon of helicopter parenting is exactly that: parents believe their children can and should do everything, and when the children fail, parents experience it, narcissistically, as a reflection of the parent (instead of a reflection of the child). Similarly, parents who expect their children to love them unconditionally and obey them always turn to violence when those expectations are not met; it is not about training the children but about expressing the narcissistically structure need for love (a gaping hole of need).

Why do we do things this way? Capitalism may be one reason.

Materialism

One answer is found in Alissa Quart's 2003 study of marketing practices and children's response to advertisements. Quart examines the promotion of pre-teenagers and teenagers from youngsters with a small allowance to the object of serious attention by youth oriented industries. Children, in Quart's view, have become major consumers, and the various corporations marketing to them have targeted these kids in a bone-chilling, calculated way. Among other things, Quart describes overt product placement in films, magazines, and video games. Worse, she describes companies such as Delia*s that encourage children to promote their products by wearing the products, talking up the products (something called "peer-to-peer marketing" [Quart 2003: 38]), and commenting on advertisement through a careful and frightening use of Web sites (17–45). Delia*s hires psychological consultants in its effort to sell more product, counting on the very real fact that American children have little if any good judgment about durable and tasteful material goods. Delia*s chooses the "cool" girls to be unpaid consultants; the girls seem not to realize that they are being shamelessly exploited.

While Delia*s marketing techniques are reprehensible in themselves, I have to wonder where the parents of these children are. Quart talked with a few parents whose children are involved with Delia*s and other teen-marketing corporations, and the overwhelming response seemed to be either that the experience was good for their daughters, since it taught the girls about marketing and fashion (apparently that's useful) or there's nothing they can do about it (38–39). But how can being involved as pawns in a cynical game of consumerism be useful for anyone? And how did parents get to be so powerless?

The psychotherapeutic metaphor is at least part of the answer. We've moved far beyond Hemingway's famous epigram that what is moral is what feels good after. We now are in Nike country, where we're supposed to "Just Do It." Forget about "Just Say No," even. If we feel like doing it, we should do it. And that applies to our children. How dare we deny them something that the children think is an expression of individuality (even if it means getting everyone to dress alike)? The parents of the children in Quart's study, as is true for most American parents, cannot tell their children "no" very often.

Indeed, we must now get instruction on saying no from advertisements ranging from Partnership for a Drug-Free America to Nesquick and from Dr. Phil to... well, Dr. Phil. For instance, in 2003, an advertisement appeared regarding drugs. A number of teenagers of all different hues appear, one after another, telling the camera how much they hated their parents for snooping into their business and, at the end of the spot, saying "Thanks." The obvious message is: parents, you really have to look after your children to make sure they're not drinking and drugging and it's okay to get in their faces! The Nesquick commercial, a little more light-hearted, involves a beautiful, smiling blond mom with three beautiful, smiling children. Mom tells her cute little girl, no, you can't wear a ballerina's outfit when we're going out to dinner; no, we aren't buying potato chips and generic grape soda; but yes! We *can* buy Nesquick you're holding since it's "healthy!" Sometimes you just have to say no to things your child wants (and notice it was the child, not the mother, who found the healthful alternative of Nesquick). Dr. Phil tells us the same thing as well, though, interestingly, he doesn't tell us how to say no (you have to buy his books to find that out, apparently).

The problem with all of this is that dominant American culture does not support authoritative (not to mention the forbidden authoritarian) figures in saying no without a good reason. In other words, adults are now bidden to present good reasons to their children for saying no. For instance, another Partnership for a Drug-Free America advertisement features a teenaged, earlobe-safety-pinned, dyed-shaved and pony-tailed-haircut-wearing, leather-clad young man (or so it appears) telling his (evidently) single mother that he's going out for the evening. Mom is concerned about who he's going out with, where he's going, and when he'll be home. He answers the questions with good grace (and with an incongruous smile given his gothic, punkish getup). Mom brushes some imaginary lint from his shoulder (or is it his safety-pinned ear?) and says okay; she doesn't tell him when to be home, notice, but lets him set that rule (and eleven o'clock, the time the boy says, seems a little late, even for a teenager). There is not a single word about the young man's appearance. The voiceover tells us to let our kids be who they are, though it appears that if they are drug-users you shouldn't let them be who they are. We are supposed to let them dress in ridiculous outfits but as long as they aren't using drugs we shouldn't care. They can express their individuality, even going so far as to pierce everything pierceable in sight as long as they stay away from the maryjane.

It's this kind of abdication of parental authority and the occasional soupçon, formerly anyway, of good taste that is led by the psychotherapeutic metaphor. Mesmerized by child development experts who tell us that it is "natural" for children to want to "express" themselves through their personal appearance, we apparently have decided that, if our children want to look a particular way as an assertion of individual identity (though, interestingly, the same kids who want to have a unique look wind up looking like all of their friends), we must let them. As Quart (2003) demonstrates, while there are a number of different "looks" out there for children, especially girls, conformity to a particular look has become essential. If a child cannot get the right shoes, or the right handbag, or the right makeup (yes, even ten- and eleven-year-olds are using makeup), she feels bad. And it is now the goal of all parents to make sure that their little angels, no matter what else happens, don't feel bad. People—her schoolmates—will make fun of her, or worse.

Although bullying is a significant problem in American schools (and elsewhere, it must be noted), the explanations for it are purely psychological—there is no larger discussion of how the behavior fits into dominant American culture and is in fact encouraged by our culture. Studies examine both the bullied and the bully. Bullies are actually very insecure children, apparently, who gain their "self-esteem" through bossing other people around. The bullied often suffer from post-traumatic stress disorder (PTSD). Both are victims, in these studies, and both need therapy. I am not minimizing some of the real physical harm inflicted by bullies. However, my generation has raised children who are as emotionally fragile and emotionally oversensitive as are their parents. As Kaminer (1993) notes, we trivialize real suffering, real anguish, and real harm by calling an overreaction to unpleasant events, including bullying, post-traumatic stress disorder. We make a mockery of those who are true victims—Rwandan mothers who have seen their families hacked to death, or inner-city children who witness the murder of their siblings by drug-running adults—when we claim that just about everyone is a victim of something. Feeling bad because someone at school teases you about your weight problem is not equivalent to the feelings of the survivors of the Bosnian genocide. Someone who was fondled, once, by a drunk uncle or the parish priest is not in the same category of sufferer as one of my family therapy clients, who was seduced into having sexual intercourse with her father starting at age eleven. Yet we seem to want to encourage a perennial sense of having been abused, of having a right to psychological bliss (occasional calm contentment, apparently, is not good enough), of never having bad, or even uncomfortable, things happen. All experiences are equivalent; all feelings are equally respectable; and all stories must be told and never judged.

Americans no longer feel it is appropriate to judge anything, particularly if behavior or thoughts are couched in the psychotherapeutic metaphor. By raising our children to think of themselves as therapy clients, and anyone they encounter as a person who must be fascinated by their interiority, we continue the narcissism embraced by the boomer generation. This is particularly true as we look at how we understand our educational system.

Chapter 5

Those Who Can't Teach

The sense of entitlement carried by young people, and the concomitant inability to recognize that they are entitled to far less than they have been led to believe, is reflected in our educational system. My generation has failed its children miserably, producing ignorant and illiterate children. Some of this effort has been well meaning if misplaced and poorly enacted cultural sensitivity, but most of it has been driven by the psychotherapeutic metaphor.

Egocentric by any other name

As noted previously in this book, the psychotherapeutic metaphor enacted in dominant American culture often is reflected in discussions of something called "self-esteem." Almost all institutions in American society today are concerned to a greater or lesser extent with self-esteem, with the possible exception of modern American and international business, commerce, and marketing. In particular, America's teachers and school administrators, and many professors of education, seem very concerned with the self-esteem of at least some of our children at least some of the time. Indeed, entire curricula are based on building the self-esteem of children, despite the fact that self-esteem (whatever that is) appears to be negatively correlated with school, social, and personal excellence.

One of the first things that should be recognized about self-esteem is that there is no operational definition of this phenomenon. It cannot be objectively measured. Any attempts at correlation between self-esteem and performance of specific tasks can be based only on self-report about how one "feels" about oneself—does a person regard herself as useful, competent, or worthwhile? Yet psychologists, social workers, and the others, many of whom have very little understanding of basic research methods (M.S.W.s, for instance, and Psy.Ds are applied degrees, with little to no reading and experience in theories and theory building), argue that self-esteem is a useful and real experience that has much to do with the social problems facing America today. Despite the clear lack of evidence connecting "healthy self-esteem" and performance in various arenas (Specht and Courtney 1994: 50–59), we continue to believe that self-esteem is a basic American right, and anything judged to harm self-esteem (whatever it is) is immoral, if not actionable.

So, for instance, textbooks prepared for schoolchildren these days are designed to enhance the self-esteem of members of every possible ethnic group who might read the books. As an example, politically conservative education historian Diane Ravitch (2003), in her examination of K-12 textbooks, notes that textbook publishers attempt to account for all ethnicities in history textbooks, sometimes with puzzling results. In discussing United States history texts, for example, Ravitch notes that

> In *Call to Freedom* and *The American Journey*, one learns of the glorious Mansa Musa, the Islamic ruler of Mali, who undertook a pilgrimage (*hajj*) to Mecca in 1324 with a grand retinue that included many thousands of slaves. Neither text explains why Mansa Musa should be considered a major figure in the history of United States, which did not exist until 450 years after his fabled *hajj*. (Ravitch 2003: 152)

Point well taken. Ravitch seems to be implying that Mansa Musa is included in a U.S. history text because both Muslims and African Americans will be reading the texts, and Mansa Musa was both Islamic and African. Despite its irrelevance, except in a tenuous, big-picture way, to U.S. history, the story of Mansa Musa seems to be included to raise the self-esteem of Muslims and children of African descent. The logic appears to be as follows: if we include historical facts about people who in part reflect the ethnicities and religious traditions of some of the students reading the book, we will be helping students understand how they fit into the material, thus raising their self-esteem. It doesn't matter if the anecdotes are actually part of the history being taught as long as children's self-esteem is raised.

Ravitch, however, can be taken seriously for only so long. She rails against the moral order being proposed by both sides of the political spectrum. Her book notes the sense of those on the Right and on the Left that books that promote either multiculturalism or Christian morality have an infectious quality: if students are exposed to a set of ideas, those ideas will deeply affect them. It must be noted that Ravitch is much more critical of the left than the right; she pays only slight attention, for example, to the attempts of fundamentalist Christians to keep science, through the teaching of evolution, out of our children's educational experience but she criticizes, in page after page, chapter after chapter, the left-leaning folks who believe that all cultures must be equally represented in textbooks. Notwithstanding that, she asserts that those who either try to influence or try to write textbooks for our children have a deep respect for the written word and apparently believe that books are so powerful as to create or negate healthy self-esteem in children. If books do not reflect a child's lived experience, the child will feel bored, or disrespected, or suicidal (I guess). Ravitch rightly points out that creating learning experiences that only reflect the child's own experiences produces a very dumb student indeed, and that learning should be not about oneself but about the world (a point reflected, surprisingly enough, in the excellent and subtle leftist works of Todd Gitlin [1995]).

What few people involved in the textbook imbroglio seem to understand is that textbooks absolutely needed revision but they do not need to reward parochialism. The noble American Indian who lived a peaceful life, respectful of nature, at least until the rotten Europeans showed up, has replaced the Great Men and Wars approach to textbook preparation. While it's true that American history does not begin in 1607 with the arrival of religious fundamentalists from England and the Netherlands, but instead begins some 20,000–40,000 years ago with the first immigrant from Siberia, celebrating American Indian ancient cultures as superior to European American culture is just plain incorrect. It appears that the production of textbooks, always a political process, has gotten completely out of hand. Ravitch argues that sometime in the past textbooks were not political and did not paint moral tales and now they do; she of course is wrong. Textbooks ignoring the realities of slavery, of the oppression of women, of the default categories of "white" and "men" against whom everyone else had to be explained, had to go and good riddance. But textbooks designed with psychological aims in mind, with therapy in mind, rather than historical accuracy, are scarcely better.

Our schools have become places where therapy rather than learning takes place, and textbooks are just one reflection of that. Given that many education majors tend to be the weakest students most non-education professors encounter (or at least this seems to be the case anecdotally), their ability to teach is questionable. Expecting them to be able to perform whatever adequate psychotherapy is possible (and that's not much, as demonstrated in chapter 2) is simply too much. At the same time, I should note that parents and families have abdicated education at home (and many other activities) and now come to expect outrageous results from overburdened, underfunded schools that are expected to do just about everything—except teach demanding material.

The pedagogy of pedagogy today seems to involve far more process than content, at least in many states and in many education programs. That is to say, college students interested in being teachers have little to no expertise in the subject areas they want to teach. College courses in pedagogy (often nicknamed "Bulletin Board 101" by more cynical professors) provide instruction in, for example, how to fill out lesson plans and how to be inclusive in the classroom. It falls to "content area" professors to provide education majors with information, analysis, and theoretical perspectives on what is to be taught—while trying to teach non-education students at the same time. Many state teachers' licensing boards have eliminated, in fact, the ability for education students to have content majors.

Illinois, for instance, redesigned its requirements to certify teachers around 2000. Its new state standards mean that students who want to be high school teachers of history or the loosely defined "social studies" (in itself a horrible conglomeration of disparate disciplines) cannot major in a specific area of study but must have what appears to be only a passing acquaintance with the following fields: history, economics, political science, psychology, sociology, anthropology, and geography. A student can no longer hope to be a biology teacher but must be ready to teach all sciences. Only in mathematics can a teacher in training hope to teach in her subject area upon certification. In addition to watered down majors (now called concentrations), education students must take a number of education courses, few of which have any content. The emphasis is on self-esteem, diversity in the classroom, and the social problems of students. Students learn various skills—learning how to listen, for instance, and creating a safe atmosphere in the classroom so that the children in the classroom can feel free to express themselves. Nowhere in the curriculum taught to education students is a sense that intellectual rigor, rather than emotional expression, might be preferable.

It may sound as though I am blaming teachers, the schools, and the education industry for all of this, and in part I am. Like other non-theoretical disciplines, education, a supremely practical profession, is not known for its intellectual acuity. Much as social workers and psychotherapists tend to work to prove the basic assumptions of their professions, education professionals are not interested in challenging the dominant paradigm. At the same time, American society has decided over the past thirty or forty years that mediocrity, produced through a lowering of standards, is fine as long as children feel good about themselves.

This attitude is troubling, to say the least. A child who believes that he is fine as he is will not struggle to become better. If you have high self-esteem, why should you bother to improve yourself? Why should you read difficult works that may challenge your sense of yourself, your place in time and space, your religious beliefs, your assumptions about how the world works? Instead, it is far more comfortable to read works by people like yourself, who confirm your point of view, who do not make you angry or upset or sad. It's much easier to find yourself in what you're exposed to instead of earning, as one student of mine memorably put it, "brain blisters." Such parochial reading can only confirm a person's sense of self-esteem. But true education and learning should be about challenging one's sense of self and one's place in the world. The promotion of self-esteem quashes any rigor in the classroom.

Not only does the emphasis on self-esteem do this. So do politicians on all levels, from the local school board to the disastrous Bush initiative, the No Child Left Behind Act.

All politics is local

It is stating the obvious, of course. School boards on the local and state level control content taught, or not taught, based on local conditions. This is the essence of the American public school system. Originally largely funded through area property taxpayers, the American school system is supposed to be flexible, dynamic, and responsive to local concerns. The system was envisioned as a way to produce educated citizens at no cost to the individual, though of course originally only male European American children of landowners were permitted to be educated to any great extent. Once childhood was thoroughly invented in the United States—roughly after the Civil War for most European American children only—the universe of children subject to public education grew until, finally, more or less after World War I most American children were expected to be in school at least until puberty. The schools were segregated and woefully underfunded in many parts of the United States (and, indeed, still are in rural areas with large African American or Appalachian populations), but they existed and they allowed for at least basic literacy and numeracy.

School boards controlled, and control, the content of education, so that there are wildly varying educational experiences. That control is largely politically motivated. So there are wide swaths of material some students never learn—evolution, sexualities, material outside the canon, recent U.S. history, current events from any standpoint but the conservative, and so forth. Some parents object to such discussions, and they insist that it is appropriate to use the Bible as part of a secular education (for instance). School boards will agree at times and thus we have our current situation, in which we have a profoundly expensive and highly ineffective educational system.

For instance, it is abundantly clear that high school students cannot write. There seems to be an increasing need for what are called developmental classes at the college level. Third-level education in the United States is being called on to provide very basic writing instruction for, often, nearly half of matriculating students. This is the kind of writing instruction—grammar, punctuation, simple sentence structure—that ought to be provided at the high school level. But because high schools today seem far more interested in helping students understand the consequences of having babies (instead of teaching them how to prevent them—another example of local control gone awry includes high schools refusing to teach students about contraception) by having them carry eggs or dolls around instead of teaching them how to write, colleges now have to make up that deficit.

Writing instruction in high school seems to follow on from reading instruction in grammar schools. While there does not seem to be a monolithic approach to reading instruction, some school systems insist on whole language reading instruction. Students are taught tricks about how to figure out what an entire word is instead of the phonics, or "sounding out," method. The latest literature seems to indicate that the whole language, or "sight-reading," approach has hurt the reading ability of a generation of young people. And it is the poster child for promoting the self-esteem movement.

The argument with this kind of reading instruction is that it is the teacher's responsibility to motivate the child to read, and that reading cannot take place unless the student enjoys it. Part of the argument for whole language instruction revolves around valuing the student's interpretation of a text and making meaning, and it is based on Chomsky's by-now unremarkable argument that language acquisition is a "hard-wired" part of human behavior. While that is indisputably accurate, reading is hardly a natural activity for humans, and making meaning of written text is rather different than making meaning of spoken words.

The problem with whole language instruction, in addition to its singular ineffectiveness, is that it privileges student meaning systems. The student becomes the arbiter of knowledge. But, remarkably, the student is so called because she doesn't actually know things. If the student knew things, she would no longer be a student. Encouraging students to decide what words mean, or what words are important, or how to pronounce words, has led to the crisis in literacy that we see today.

Furthermore, the whole language system decries phonics as "boring." Apparently children are not to be bored and it seems that they cannot tolerate boredom. I guess as well children are not to be taught that sometimes one must recite and repeat and memorize in order to acquire skills. No, instead, the child-centered curriculum (instead of a knowledge-centered curriculum) abdicates to childish tastes and abilities. The childish perspective is privileged and a yearning toward adult activities is indulged without children actually having to work.

The point is not that children should be expected to sit still for eight hours a day; that is not expected of adults either. But assuming that children cannot learn through recitation, that repetition is by its nature counterproductive to learning, and that children should not have to learn how to deal with boredom is all tied up with the quite indulgent cultural philosophy we have toward children today (or, at least, some children; see chapter 6 for another picture of a different set of children).

We are to create systems of instruction that are fun and not boring, ever, and that encourage children to offer opinions on subjects about which they know little. Children are encouraged, through whole language pedagogy (which seems to have spread its ideological tentacles in many other areas), to focus on themselves, on their reactions, on their meanings. Once again hyperindividualism has reared its ugly head, and children are being taught to learn only in ways that are intrinsically meaningful to them, instead of learning meanings that others—adults, experts, authorities in the area—have decided are accurate. No, we can't do that. That would be boring.

It is profoundly disappointing that most schools (through twelfth grade) are not in fact teaching the 3Rs. Part of the resistance to reading and writing (and, I guess, 'rithmetic) is this completely irrelevant and unproven hypothesis that people have different learning styles and the educational system must cater to them rather than insisting that students cater to the educational system. So we get (for instance) Sesame Street, which taught kids that Learning.

Is. Fun. Well, no, it isn't. Not all of the time, anyway. Sometimes it's boring. Sometimes it's unpleasant. Sometimes you have to slog through a load of nonsense to get to the one gem you might find all day. Bringing in electronic media as anything but a special treat (anyone else remember film strips with the record albums that dinged and often skipped?) is helping encourage the view that learning ought to be fun first and foremost and that learning has to be individualized—by the teacher, not by the individual—so that in fact the system has changed profoundly. Rather than insisting on a particular body of knowledge is to be—yes—memorized, "educators" insist that "active learning" is more important. This means that students decide what is interesting and important.

Well, forgive me, but students are by definition ignorant. They do not get to make that decision. This is a major difference from the original system. Students and parents rather than the actual possessors of knowledge and information decide what is to be learned because, after all, they're paying our salaries. (I mean all of us who teach in public venues when I say "our" and "we.") So we get the horror of "teaching the controversy" when there isn't one (at least, there is no scientific controversy about evolution), for instance, because that's what parents, who apparently are not all that bright themselves, want.

Knowing things is now devalued; knowing how to do things properly is ridiculed since, after all, we destroyed authority a while ago and anyway who are we to assert any knowledge since our students know as much as we do; demanding that students demonstrate knowledge is hurtful to self-esteem. That's on the one hand; on the other hand are the idiotic national tests that prove nothing about knowledge and a great deal about the ability of folks to find ways to cheat.

And, yes, I know, there are students who have learning differences who even twenty years ago might have been left in a special ed. classroom to rot. What disturbs me is that so many students now are "diagnosed" (via very dubious means) with learning disabilities that explain their lack of performance. It comes down to being able to demonstrate ability, ultimately. We need to come to grips with that throughout the system, including those children with learning differences.

Students are also indulged, through what is a growing movement never to offend anyone, in avoiding learning things that they argue offend their basic beliefs. Young people are not actually knowledgeable enough to say so in this country, when adolescence these days seems to end around thirty, that learning about things like evolution or other forms of religious belief is offensive, and that they do not have an obligation to sit in classes that offend them. But teachers, principals, school boards, and parents all agree that students should not be offended. Parents also work hard ensuring that they and their parenting is neither criticized nor offended.

We now seem to be in a cultural location in which we can never be challenged. Parents assert their rights to prevent their children from learning about things that may contradict the parents' religious beliefs. Indeed, the thinly disguised creationism of intelligent design masquerades as "science" in some curricula; parents assert that they are entitled to insist that students be "taught the controversy" of evolution. Despite the fact that there is little scientific controversy surrounding evolution, somehow this discussion, coming from non-experts, has gained some traction. Since all offensive items are to be removed from the curriculum, whether they have to do with religious variety, scientific fact, or historical realities, principals and school boards agree. Students then are taught close to nothing and come to college woefully deficient in a number of knowledge suites.

As mentioned above, students are not challenged to learn how to write. Following on from whole language instructions, students are encouraged in high schools to write papers about how they feel about things (there's that psychotherapeutic metaphor again!) as a way for them to make meaning. Again, there is nothing particularly natural about reading and writing, though there certainly is a basic human tendency to learn to speak in a holistic and meaning-making way. Education pedagogy, though, currently insists that schoolchildren have valid and important voices to which we must pay heed, and, in the current cultural climate, parents insist that their children's unique voices must be heard.

What a cacophony those voices make. How exactly is a principal with integrity or a school board with true interest in student learning supposed to respond to competing interest groups? They are supposed to teach science but not teach science; they are supposed to teach some histories but not others; they are supposed to support some sexualities but not others; they are, above all, supposed to make sure that students are happy and engaged in learning things that are individually tailored to each student. And education pedagogy has only encouraged this trend, by moving the teacher away from the realm of disciplinary expert and into the fuzzy world of promoting self-esteem. When children are being encouraged to consider their needs first, their interests first, their interpretations first, how on earth can any common learning take place?

What we get instead is a new set of ideas about learning. The "student as customer" philosophy of educational structure, both at the K-12 level and, increasingly, at the college level, means that students determine what they will learn, not the experts in teaching a particular subject. If a student faces a challenge to his ideas about how the world works, he is often supported in opting out from learning things by his parents. Indeed, his parents may insist that the school has no right to contradict their religious teachings. Alternatively, parents may insist that a school has no right to ask a child to say the Pledge of Allegiance, with its 1950s-imposed reference to God (as a way to fight the Commies, who, apparently, were godless), contradicting their atheist teachings (as a recent California case asserted, ultimately unsuccessfully). Parents lately insist that their unique, wonderful children must be treated with kid gloves, with great patience, and with indulgence so that their special specialness can emerge.

This seems true whether the special specialness actually involves talent or is uninteresting or unethical. Lately students who plagiarize—who engage in intellectual theft—are not disciplined but allowed to continue with their educational careers (and high school teachers who insist on prosecuting plagiarism may find themselves out of a job). Parents insist that intellectual theft is a mistake, or unimportant, or is the school's fault; what it never is, for many parents, is their children's fault. The deliberate cutting and pasting of sources, the clearly meant copying of someone else's work, is not to be punished, for many parents. Instead of having actual consequences from school systems, parents want their misbehaving children to be given chance after chance after chance. What then do young people learn? That they can behave in unethical ways and get away with it, largely.

Consider the experience of a school superintendent in Sacramento, California, in 2001. Dr. Peter Mehas refused to allow plagiarists to graduate high school; he imposed serious consequences on cheaters. And parents' responses to his assertions that this behavior is unacceptable involve providing excuses for the young people: "they didn't cite things correctly" or "it was just a little bit of plagiarism" (Hafner 2001). Not many school boards will support such a response to plagiarism, though.

Tiny Piper, Kansas, insisted that a teacher who caught twenty-eight students in a cheating ring and failed them had to change the grades to passing. Parents seem to think that failing a course because students steal other people's words is too extreme a response. One parent, whose child apparently was not part of the cheating, said the following:

> "If your boss said to you, 'You were late one day this month so we're not going to pay you for the whole month,' is that fair?" asked Mary Myer, whose son, Mitchell, was not accused of cheating. "Plagiarism is not a cut-and-dried issue," she added. "Somebody who gets in their car and hurts someone, we punish them differently than someone who goes out and shoots someone. Intent matters." (Wilgoren 2001)

Ms. Myer seems fundamentally unaware of the ethical implications of this kind of cheating. It is not equivalent to being late to work one day. It is equivalent, instead, to taking credit for your colleagues' work without their permission, being paid for that work—the work that you have not done—and representing yourself as more knowledgeable about a subject than you really are.

And, while it is true to some extent that "intent matters," it is probably stretching credulity a bit to argue that plagiarists who cut and paste paragraphs, pages, or whole chapters do not mean to do that. They are copying someone else's words and representing them as their own. They may assert that they did not intend to cheat, but it is hard to know what else to call the deliberate highlighting of some text from a website and copying it onto your own blank page without attribution. It is intellectual thievery and it is something that occurs more and more.

Now, part of this particular educational problem is exacerbated by the nature of the Internet, which allows the kind of editorial activity described above. Certainly the Internet's constant availability can tempt all kinds of people—including those who ought to know better, like Doris Kearns Goodwin—to cut and paste particularly pithy quotes or delightfully amusing sections of prose. But simply because one is tempted does not mean one gives into temptation. And this is at the heart of the problem.

While the actual activity of plagiarism is bad enough in and of itself, it speaks to a larger cultural problem. As I have been arguing throughout this book, American culture encourages a continual self-monitoring, taking one's emotional pulse throughout the day. So if you feel like cutting and pasting someone else's words, it's okay if you don't actually mean to steal them. How does one can solve the logical problem here—cutting and pasting, and inserting that cut and paste into your text, is by its very nature stealing? Perhaps since the person doesn't think it's stealing, then it isn't stealing.

But plagiarism is bad. This requires some old-fashioned language, such as "honorable behaviors" and "integrity." As educated people, all we have are our minds and our ideas, which we express with our words. If I cannot trust that your words are indeed your words, I cannot trust you or the worth of your education. You then are unemployable to me. Since a degree, and especially a college degree, gives us the chance to go beyond putting widgets into gadgets (indeed, pretty much precludes that kind of work), we must be able to demonstrate that we have the skills and the talents and the knowledge to do the work for which we are hired. If the skills and talents and knowledge are obtained fraudulently, there is no point to education. Many parents, though, believe that such a stance is far too harsh, at least when applied to their children.

And so another part of the larger cultural problem is connected to our current child-rearing philosophy. Children are viewed as wonderful unique beings whose self-esteem is crucial to protect and who cannot be ever told no. Their every utterance is greeted with respect and enthrallment. This keeps us from feeling comfortable in judging bad behavior as bad. We've taught our kids that all emotions are valid, and that there is no such thing as bad, and that judging is wrong (only we call it being judgmental). So if the student just has a good reason for cheating, no one understands—students, parents, and some of our colleagues—why we shouldn't "understand," forgive, and allow a do-over.

The behavior is thievery, and parents are far less understanding of other children's crimes and difficulties (see chapter 6). Instead of insisting on adherence to a minimal moral code that acknowledges one's responsibility to the greater good—as adhering to a no-cheating honor code demands—parents want their children forgiven over and over and over and over again. But they want other children—usually, children of color—punished to the fullest extent of the law when those other children violate laws. Parents demanding a second bite at the honesty apple for their children find that children on welfare, or in foster care, or otherwise troubled, are not worthy of that second bites for those children. The insistence that their children are deserving of second chances, but other children are not, is a moral horror and a shameful position. Parents of cheaters need to start punishing their children and stop punishing those children who truly are suffering. Parents also need to start limiting less difficult but still unhelpful behavior. Privileging the utility of "multi-tasking," for instance, is yet another instance of lowest-common-denominator thinking.

Multitasking is a chimera and we need to stop encouraging it or, at least, tolerating it in our students. As those who hire our young people will confirm, and, indeed, as those who work in the "real world" will as well, the notion that multitasking is a good thing is wrong. Concentration remains a major requirement for many jobs that our young people will take; and, in addition, multitasking in the presence of others is just plain rude. Students who text-message during dinner, who think it's appropriate to IM, watch television, listen to music, and hold a conversation, are doing many things, none of them well. Students (especially those who do poorly) must turn off the television, the computer, the iPod, the radio, the cell phone, and so on when studying. Go to the library. Go to the dining hall. But get away from the electronics and focus.

Not only do students fail to learn how to write in high school, as discussed before, and adopt multitasking as though it's a legitimate learning modality, but reading in general also seems to be seen as an old-fashioned, boring activity, since it is not filled with choppy camera angles and moody, bass-filled music. Reading actually requires some quiet and some concentration, and American culture today has produced a rather large group of folks, across generations, who seem terrified of quiet. It seems as though fewer and fewer people find reading compelling. One cannot be a competent writer without having read loads and loads and loads of stuff—good and bad. It therefore does not surprise me that there are such lousy writers in our college classes—certainly high schools have demanded little good writing (and that in itself is not a great surprise given the quality of education majors). But in a larger sense, we have abandoned the physical written word, forsaking it for flashy graphics and peppy music on the Web.

Furthermore, the "everyone is unique and wonderful" child-rearing philosophy, coupled with the overly egalitarian notion that college is for everyone at whatever time they choose to attend, is hurting true liberal arts education and, at the same time, hurting true vo-tech training. College is designed, correctly, to produce educated citizens (the U.S. public educational system was supposed to do that through high school but, as we know, self-esteem rather than reading hard things thoroughly seems to be the value in high school these days); vo-techs produce, well, technicians. That latter thing is fine; it just isn't college, yet it's being asked in some ways to step in for it, particularly at the community colleges.

The solution is to fix high school so that young people regardless of track (vocational or prep, though it isn't clear how salient those distinctions are any longer) can read at a reasonable level (say, tenth grade), can do competent arithmetic, some algebra (for the abstract thought part of it), and some geometry. This means changing the way we do teacher education—which lately has included just about the worst students in the college. Teacher education must be focused on content areas rather than methods. We have non-experts or even non-not-even-familiar-with-the-subject new teachers teaching things they know nothing about; that needs to change!

And, for a thoroughly frightening take on this, see the *New York Times* Education section recently, in which a celebratory article discusses the admission of Downs' Syndrome students to college. To *college*! The mother of one of the Downs' Syndrome students apparently believes her son is entitled to go to college:

> "He always wanted to go to college, and this new program was the perfect opportunity to get the support he needed," says his mother, Susan McCormack. She doesn't think her goals for his education are unachievable. "My hope is that he will get a little out of an education and make some contacts," she says, "maybe get a job, make friends and have new experiences....He might not get the full value that a normal child would, but he still deserves the opportunity to get as much as he can and learn as much as he can," Mrs. McCormack says. "It is something we are willing to do to help him to get to his potential." (Kaufman 2006)

The hubris here is just astounding. How on earth does a child with such significant learning problems "deserve" to go to college, taking up a space that might be occupied by someone who might learn something? If the point of sending a child with Downs' Syndrome to college is to allow that child to make friends and have experiences, aren't there less expensive and more appropriate places for McCormack's son to go? This is the entitlement culture gone far, far awry. Because her son wants to go to college, despite the absurdity of the entire enterprise in this situation, this mother insists that he has a right to do so. I suppose she also will protest any grade below an A as well, since her son is wonderful and talented and unique. Any attempt to expect an A to mean excellent will be squashed.

That's the way I am

Parents beyond Mrs. McCormack clearly collude in the suppression of excellence. By believing that their children are unique personalities from birth (or beforehand; see chapter 2), parents help their children make excuses for poor performance even as the schools lower standards further and further. An entire industry has arisen centered on different "learning styles" and the apparent explosion in the diagnosis of mental illness among children (including, according to a recent *Time* report, seriously underreported bipolar disorder in teenagers [Kluger 2003: 48–58]). Parents, seeing their children get dumber and dumber, agree that the psychotherapeutic metaphor, with its self-esteem and emotional expression and acceptance of "differences," is far more useful than expecting a certain minimal behavioral and educational standard.

The burgeoning discussion of "learning styles"—which are taught to education students as real—provide an on-point example. Professionals engaged in discussions of children—education professors, psychologists, social workers, counselors, and the like—assert that each of us is born with a particular learning style. Pedagogy aimed at only one kind of instruction, usually lecture or lecture/discussion, is singled out as harmful to the self-esteem of students who embody different ways of learning. Some of us, it is asserted (with absolutely no reliable proof), are visual learners—we have to see the principle enacted before we understand it. Some of us are kinetic learners—we have to perform the principle before we can get it (a bit difficult to do with, for instance, subatomic physics). Others of us are auditory learners—we have to hear something before we understand it. Still others are emotional learners—we must be able to incorporate a principle emotionally before we can comprehend it. And there are other learning styles. Teachers must accommodate all learning styles in the classroom, or those who are not "able" to incorporate material through lecture and discussion will be harmed, as will their self-esteem. These students are otherly abled and must be provided for.

It is not clear that catering to "different learning styles" to the extent many of those writing about teaching counsel us to do is a great idea. This will not prepare students for the world of work, where it does not matter what your learning style is. Get the report in, and do it yesterday. Complete the spreadsheet regardless of whether you prefer the kinetic form of learning. We can assume, anyway, that almost everyone is proficient in at least two and often more learning styles, and everyone really ought to be able to learn in many ways.

We need to be showing students that they will be expected to conform to the dominant learning styles of this culture, those of verbal, visual, and reading (depending of course on the discipline being discussed). While accommodations to true learning differences are important, motivational or impulse control issues (which, face it, just about every adolescent has) are not learning differences. If our school systems, whether elementary, high school, or college are allowing such things, perhaps there needs to be a culture-wide discussion about whether these are legitimate learning problems. We need to stop medicalizing poor behavior.

Nowhere in any of these discussions is the notion that we should hold children—and all Americans, for that matter, at least those not demonstrably neurologically damaged—to a standard higher than that which defines them at the moment. Of course children who can't read should not be expected to read material in order to understand it—but children should be taught how to read. Television should have no part of that equation, by the way. Television, a visual medium, cannot teach children how to concentrate. Indeed, it destroys concentration. Children who are kinetic learners must learn other ways of learning. One cannot understand abstract ideas through enacting them. It simply doesn't work. One must think. We should be encouraging children to have a variety of learning styles. We must stop asserting that there are different, inborn learning styles that cannot be changed. If someone is primarily visually oriented, fine. But that person must learn other ways that encourage literacy, discourage self-centeredness, and challenge the student rather than allowing him to say "that's just how I am." (And it is more than a little disconcerting to hear a fourteen-year-old make pronouncements about his personality. A fourteen-year-old is not finished, and suggesting that he can argue that his personality is set in stone is about the worst thing adults can allow.)

In addition to empirically untenable ideologies of learning styles, the psychopharmaceutical industry in many ways has helped, with the clever use of the psychotherapeutic metaphor, to create the diagnosis of Attention Deficit Hyperactivity Disorder, or ADHD, and its companion, Attention Deficit Disorder, or ADD. No longer confined to children, apparently, millions of Americans seemingly suffer from an inability to concentrate. We need, of course, to be medicated.

There are many ways to understand the prevalence of ADHD today, but none of them are medical, and few of them are psychological or neurological (at any rate, no biological or psychological connection has been convincingly demonstrated). Rather, we need to look at American culture and the crisis the Baby Boomer generation has helped to construct for its children. For instance, as mentioned previously, many parents are working at least two jobs (oftentimes more than that) in order to buy houses that are far beyond their means (or needs, for that matter—what does a family of three need with a four bedroom house?). That obviously is not the case for the poor and the working poor of this country. But for the middle and upper middle classes, work is important partly for itself and partly to buy stuff—stuff like four bedroom houses, SUVs (again, what does a family of three need with an SUV?), fancy furniture, and private schools. Such behavior teaches children many things, none of them good: if I want something, I get to have it right away; televisions in every room are a basic human right; every child is entitled to a computer; I get to consume resources far beyond my needs. These are profoundly immoral lessons.

Instead of providing time, parents today provide stuff. And when they get home from working to accumulate all that stuff, they want a calm, peaceful atmosphere. Excited, boisterous, noisy children—the very children that my generation's child-rearing methods have encouraged to develop—are precisely not what are desired. How to handle the child, excited to see guests, without upsetting tired parents? Ritalin. But medicating normal American childish behavior is simply unconscionable.

Yet that is what we're doing. At last count, some 5 million children, largely boys, were taking Ritalin. While Ritalin does, in some mysterious way, seem to calm active behavior, we seem uninterested in getting at the root of the behavior. It surely could be—and has been—argued that the rise in the diagnosis (such a scientific sounding word for a very fuzzy practice) of ADHD and ADD is directly related to the growing size of classrooms. However, there is a flaw in that argument: most Boomers attended schools with an average class size of forty-five, and ADHD was as yet "undiscovered." So class size by itself is not enough to explain the drugging of America's children.

Instead, a cultural explanation seems much more viable. The ubiquity of television, for instance, clearly is connected with a growing inability to concentrate. Although recent studies indicate that children are actually watching less television these days, it is frightening to note that those same studies show that children are spending more time at the computer both on the Web and playing computer games. With instant access, bright graphics that move and squiggle, and often poorly written text in Web sites, children (and adults) seem to be incapable of concentration any longer. So one part of the puzzle with regard to ADHD is that parental affluence (or, at the least, a credit line) allows children access to electronic media that is primarily a passive experience. Once away from the video screen, children who had been quiet all of a sudden are making noise. That seems to be troublesome for parents.

In addition to the mere existence of television and other electronic media, a cultural change of some magnitude has taken place. Children and young adults seem to be incapable of sitting still for something that they perceive as boring. If a teacher isn't zingy, with lots of video and PowerPoints and other electronic playthings, children get bored, it seems (there are those learning styles again!). In fact, a teacher who emphasizes lecture or lecture/discussion over "inter-active" activities (though it's hard to know how a discussion isn't interactive) is criticized (Peshkin 1994: 121). Teachers are expected now to entertain students. Style over substance is the key here—and recall that teachers are no longer required to be expert in subject areas. No wonder Johnny can't read.

The quick changing nature of electronic media has encouraged a lack of concentration on the part of children. Rather than combating that flaw by demanding concentration from children, we have caved in to it. We now cater for the child who can't concentrate—indeed, concentration and discipline seem to be foreign concepts (except, perhaps, in sports, hardly an important intellectual activity). So what we have produced are many, many children who cannot concentrate—we medicate those who are the worst, the most uncontrollable, with drugs with no provenance and no history. But our society is ADHD—and we've allowed it.

The content of our character

Sort of. Along with the widespread disbursement of psychotropic drugs for what are actually culturally induced behaviors, educators have now decided that something called "character development" should take pride of place in our schools. Even a cursory glance at some of this clearly ideologically induced propaganda should frighten Americans. As Kohn perceptively demonstrates, those pushing character development in schools have a profoundly conservative, if not fundamentalist, agenda (Kohn 2003: 102–117). Nowhere, for instance, in the Character Counts! Web site (www.goodcharacter.com) is there any discussion of larger social issues. Instead, various lessons for elementary, middle, and high school students emphasize the importance of taking responsibility for your behavior, turning in those who don't behave well, being patriotic, and acknowledging your feelings. Nowhere is there a call for social action against poverty, for instance. Nowhere is there a discussion of how to get corporate America out of your school (indeed, those few brave students who have protested the sponsorship of Coke—including hallway banners in addition to soda machines—e.g., have been harshly disciplined [Ravitch 2003]). Character development appears to be supremely individualized, aimed at keeping order in school but certainly not interested in producing students who can think dispassionately or analyze critically. It is but a reflection of the moral paucity of American culture today.

Just desserts

As discussed before, the idea has somehow emerged that college is an entitlement, that all young people in America must go to college or be read as failures. We have children suffering from severe developmental delays, with Downs' Syndrome, going to college because they want to. We have children who have little interest, if any, in learning much going to college because the B.A. has become the only pathway to financial success. We have woefully underprepared and unmotivated young people going to college, taking out loans, and choosing to do little of interest with the privilege of a college education. Many young people in college today aren't ready for it. But they've been reared with the notion that everything they do is wonderful and fabulous and that, with just a little effort, they too can be president (or get an A).

The point here is not to tell your kids that they are worthless and weak. The point is to let them know that the world is not filled with unlimited possibilities, that someone who cannot sing worth a damn shouldn't aim to be an opera singer or that a kid who is moderately good at baseball still won't have a real shot at the majors. Parents who encourage their kids to believe they can excel at everything are harming their kids. I'm not saying that parents shouldn't encourage their kids to try whatever interests them (and parents should encourage their kids to try things that don't interest them...like, oh, perhaps math or brussels sprouts). But encouraging kids to think that they are marvelous and wonderful at everything, if they just only make a little effort, is not a great idea. Many students in college today think they can do anything, and they can do it easily, and that their effort—not their output, but their effort—is all that counts.

Well, effort means little in the end. Results are what count, and kids who are being told they are wonderful at everything and deserve to be treated as such, kids who are being treated as the center of the universe, are being done a great disservice. The world will disabuse them of these notions. Everyone can't be the center of the universe. All of us must sacrifice time and attention and, sometimes, money to make society work. A society filled with narcissists will be a Hell; we're halfway there as it is.

All things to all people

American society has in essence abandoned its commitment to education. We no longer expect our teachers to actually know anything about the subjects they are assigned to teach. But we do expect our schools to engage in character development, to diagnose mental illness, to help children express their feelings, to increase a child's self-esteem, to provide psychotherapeutic services, to encourage service learning, to assist children in becoming techno-savvy, to feed children, to provide corporations with lifelong customers through corporate sponsorship of schools, to provide a multicultural education (taught by people who know little of the world beyond their immediate area with few exceptions), to be sensitive to religious fundamentalists who aim to take over our public schools. We are expecting far too much out of people who themselves are educated very poorly. Someone with a B.A. in education is highly unlikely to know much about anything, much less all of the things listed above. We as a society have caved in to low expectations, to practical rather than intellectual training of teachers, to parents too busy to parent their children and to extended families who seem to care little for their relatives. We have, just about all of us, become teenagers—we want a lot but don't want to have to do anything to achieve. We want to start in the middle and work our way up. If we're bored, we want to change the channel—and we're teaching that to our kids. Indeed, there is a class of children with whom this society is supremely bored: those enmeshed in the child welfare system. It is to that mess we go next.

Chapter 6

The Sacrifice of Our Children

It would not be an exaggeration to say (particularly but not only through an examination child welfare system and our child-rearing practices) that America's treatment of children is a clear outlier in terms of our treatment of children. Our child welfare system is appallingly cruel, highly inefficient, and less than unconcerned with the fate of its clients—American children. Due in large part to the unquestioning allegiance to the psychotherapeutic metaphor, otherwise well-intentioned adults sacrifice, experiment on, or assist in the deaths of, our children. Other factors come into play as well: the incredible selfishness of the American taxpayer, leading to massive underfunding of various state and federal programs meant to "save" children; hyperindividualism arising from the psychotherapeutic metaphor, helping most Americans to regard the child welfare system, and children in general apart from their own (and sometimes their own children), as nothing to do with them; a grossly unfair and discriminatory economic system, encouraging Americans to believe, incorrectly, that all they have to do is try and abundant and deserved happiness will burst upon them like a welcome summer shower.

Even those politicians who claim to care about American families clearly couldn't care less—for instance, former senator Bob Barr (R-GA), a main sponsor of the contradictory and difficult "Defense of Marriage Act" in 1996 apparently believes so much in marriage that he's done it four times. Yet he would like to control the marital practices of each citizen of each of the fifty states. The former House leader, Newt Gingrich (R-GA) (why are these folks all hailing from Georgia?), a strong believer in making divorce far less accessible, is on wife number three, having left his first wife and their children when the first wife was in the hospital recovering from breast cancer, and having abandoned wife number two for a much younger woman (apparently an intern); it turns out that he was having an affair with an intern at exactly the same time he was trying to impeach Bill Clinton for lying about the very same thing.

If politicians truly cared about children and families in America, they would be fighting for increased funding for child welfare systems across the country; they would be fighting to increase the minimum wage so that families could remain together earning a living wage; they would be fighting for a cap on profits and arguing for a cessation in excessive and federally subsidized marketing of products that serve little to no purpose (Big Macs, for instance). Politicians would be interested in encouraging the growth of community; they would help all of us take responsibility for each other; they would understand and communicate the importance of the duties and obligations we have toward each other. But few if any are actually interested in being leaders; they are interested in being politicians. And so they, and we, have abandoned our children even as we act more childishly every day.

Handing out whuppings

Americans don't quite know what to do with abuse. On the one hand, just about everyone claims to be the adult victim/survivor of something. Some claim that their parents were "emotionally abusive," since their parents yelled at them and sometimes belittled their efforts. Some claim that their parents were "physically abusive," since their parents slapped them now and then. Some claim that they are "adult children of parental alienation syndrome" (Baker 2007). Some claim that their parents either were "sexually abusive" or allowed "sexual abuse," since a butt was pinched or a breast fondled. While I do not condone any of these child-rearing behaviors—belittling children, slapping children, attempting to turn children against one or the other parent, or fondling children are actions of morons—these behaviors in no way are abusive.

Abuse takes place when a biological father initiates intercourse with his eleven-year-old daughter. Abuse takes place when a mother knocks out her six-year-old's teeth for sassing back. Abuse takes place when a parent, clearly psychotic, refuses help of any kind and raises a psychotic child. What happens when we lump all abuse into one category, so that each action has caused the same kind of hurt, shame, and difficulty, is that the category itself becomes irrelevant; we become desensitized to the horror of real abuse.

And so what we see is a certain impatience when hearing about abuse. Because all abuse is equivalent, those children in real, imminent danger are treated the same as those adults who might have had an unpleasant though isolated experience. We also seem to believe that children who were abused grow up to become abusers, despite the amazing lack of empirical, objective evidence proving this. Certainly we have the potential to parent as we were parented; but if our culture did not provide encouragement for the impulsiveness, narcissism, and childishness that tends to underlie most parental abusive behavior, true abuse cases would be far less frequent. However, because, again, just about every person is the victim or survivor of abuse of some kind, due in large part to our acceptance of adult impulsiveness, narcissism, and childishness in general, abusive behavior is simply encouraged by American dominant culture.

Another factor comes into play here. Americans have a curiously naïve belief that children belong to parents, that the fact of biological parenthood somehow trumps all but the most physically damaging behavior. Parents who abandon their children for days or weeks at a time, parents who truly physically harm their children, parents who sexually assault their children, are treated by America's child welfare system as equivalent to parents who leave a child overnight in the care of a neighbor, or parents who spank their children, or parents who breastfeed their children beyond age three. In most states, families who come to the attention of state child welfare officials and who are judged to be abusive or neglectful are provided with what are called intensive services. They may receive anger management classes or parenting classes (usually ten relatively brief sessions each; neither of these programs has any empirical validity). Perhaps they'll be subject to brief therapy of one kind or another (again, there is no evidence that therapy helps anyone get over anything). Homemakers may come to visit; a homemaker is a minimum-wage state-worker who is supposed to help the parent client be a better household manager but usually does all the work herself. There might be sporadic visits, if the client is lucky, from a state social worker, and juvenile or family court monitoring (most families must report to juvenile or family court every three or six months for a progress report). While these services do cost money, though not all that much, and much is made of them by state child welfare officials, there is absolutely no evidence that any of them, singly or in combination, work.

It appears that, by an overwhelming reliance on the psychotherapeutic metaphor, and a concomitant refusal to place parents' (and children's) behavior in overt moral terms, child welfare officials simply enable—to use an overused term—parents to continue to engage in abusive behavior. The emphasis on fixing poor parenting, rather than a highly defective culture and an immoral economic system, both of which exacerbate abusive inclinations, ensures that children will continue to be beaten, belittled, and fondled by parents and relatives (and strangers, for that matter). Fixing the parents is simply not enough, and it doesn't work anyway. Bringing in extended family is unlikely to be helpful, by the way: grandparents are the ones who reared the parents, after all. Why should they be expected to do any better simply because they've aged a little bit? There is little inducement, though, in our society, for child welfare officials, families, parents, and the rest of us to step up and say: this is not working. We are helping to murder our children.

For child welfare officials, timidity and wholesale acceptance of the psychotherapeutic metaphor is the order of the day. Despite the tenuous grasp of any empirical validity of their asserted solutions to the problems of abuse, social workers, psychologists, therapists, counselors, and the rest of the mental health industry simply cannot take the necessary wider view. Psychotherapy does not work. But for those committed to its practice, saying so would be tantamount to abandoning all hope of earning any decent living. Most child welfare "reforms" do not involve the loss of jobs for anyone, including the juvenile court lawyers, judges, clerks, and bailiffs; most certainly the therapists and social workers cannot admit that their efforts are in vain because they are aiming at the wrong target. Social change is not part of the psychotherapeutic metaphor. It's too hard. At least you see the individual person sitting across from you in your therapist's office.

So instead of significant and lasting overhauls of the child welfare system, we get tinkering. Family preservation was shown to be completely ineffectual—so the state of Illinois decided to go the intensive services route. While the state was pleased at the admittedly huge reduction in the foster-care rolls, there is no evidence that children are actually better off. The state is mandated to make a decision about parental rights nine months after an abuse case is founded, or declared by the Illinois Department of Children and Family Services (DCFS) to have enough factual evidence to be true. DCFS social workers have to decide relatively quickly whether intensive services to an abusive family are working; if they are not (if, for instance, another report of abuse is called in to the central hotline), social workers have to decide whether the children must be removed from the home and put into foster care. If the child is going to foster care, social workers must then decide whether the child will be provided with kin care—foster care provided by relatives of the abusive parent, often grandparents (Welch 2003: 4–5)—stranger care or residential care, all of which are paid for largely by state and federal tax monies. Kin care is the cheapest (though some legislators think relatives should not be paid at all for caring for their kin [Franck 2003: C1, C6]), while residential care is the most expensive.

A number of questions come to mind when considering this system, which is supposed to be in the best interests of the child. First, we have to ask why the child, rather than the parent(s), is removed from the home. Why do not foster parents move into the family home? After all, it is not the child who has been abusive; it has been the parents. Yet it is the child who is punished, who is taken from her belongings, her school, her siblings, her home. The short answer, of course, is that foster parents do not want to disrupt their lives, their homes. It is far easier to move the child than the parent (there are some innovative programs in which the child remains in the neighborhood, though not in her house; see Murphy 1998a, 1998b). There is no sound therapeutic reason for this (if there were sound therapeutic reasons for anything, that is). There is no sound justice system reason for this, except that parents might then be considered a flight risk or some such nonsense (why should they submit to state oversight if the state can temporarily take their homes?). There is no sound social work reason for this. Quite simply, the foster care solution is the easiest but probably nearly the worst solution to an immediate situation of abuse in the home—the worst solution, of course, would be to do what this country did for close to 200 years: we ignored abuse entirely. But how can those who claim both to care about children and to be experts in their care settle for such an imperfect, even harmful, response to the physical and sexual abuse of children?

The psychotherapeutic metaphor makes it possible. By providing clearly impoverished responses to abusive situations, by providing "services" that do no good and in fact do significant harm (by continuing a narcissistic, apolitical, apparently amoral, and overly individualistic emphasis), child welfare experts are showing their true stripes. They do not in fact care about children. They care about being experts. They care about looking as though they know something about children.

However, like most Americans, those who claim expertise in child development are ignorant of child-rearing methods beyond the United States. Lately social work schools, among other mental health training schools, include what they call classes in cultural diversity. But the material does not go outside the United States, and "other" cultures are discussed in the context of an unexamined but apparently "true" American dominant culture. There are few involved in the psychotherapeutic industry who actually understand another society and its culture. How can they interrogate their own, or incite students to do the same?

All of this shows that far being the child development experts they claim to be, child welfare workers and administrators are woefully underprepared to deal with child abuse in the United States. By accepting without question the psychotherapeutic metaphor, psychologists, social workers, and other mental health "professionals" actively harm children and their families. They are part of an abusive system; and they get very mad when their expertise is challenged!

Somebody else's children

Foster care, then, is used to cope with child abuse. It is used in other circumstances as well, of course. Children are placed in foster care if their parents have substance abuse problems, or if parents are judged to be incompetent due to what is deemed serious mental illness, or if parents abandon their children, or if children simply become uncontrollable. We could even consider the placement of children on psychiatric wards as a form of foster care. The alleged experts take over parenting for those who seem unable to cope. Indeed, many inpatient psychiatric programs for anorexics (for instance) allow for only limited contact between parents and children for a year—the "experts" apparently believe that, all evidence to the contrary, anorexics suffer from an interiority rather than a family problem (Gremillion 2003: 74–75). It is largely the children in foster care who receive psychotherapeutic treatment, not the parents. The extended family, the neighborhood, the community apparently are not connected to symptomatic behavior of children.

Foster care is largely foisted on poor folks, and its psychotherapeutic nature cannot be refused. Even though the services provided to parents are far less onerous than those imposed on children, the continual message here is that the parents have screwed up, the children are screwed up, and nobody else has anything to do with it. The most well-intentioned social worker in the world will still exhibit smiley faces and frowny faces while trying to fix one family at time. Instead of organizing neighborhoods and communities into functioning areas, social workers and others in the child welfare system chime in with sonorous pronouncements about the growing problem of, say, bipolar disorder in children (Kluger and Song 2002; Kluger

2003). Instead of looking at the frenetic electronic world in which most of us live today as correlated with increasingly manic and out-of-control behavior by today's teens, medication is prescribed. Child welfare experts really seem to know very little about what's causing the increase in ADD and ADHD, or bipolar disorder, or autism, or in general a strong sense of unhappiness in American children.

The connection does not seem to be drawn between the psychotherapeutic metaphor, an intense narcissism and materialism, encouragement of emotional expressiveness (rather than courtesy and good manners), and children who car-jack and murder just because they were bored, as seems to be happening on an increasing basis. We seem to be unable to see that murder for the thrill of it is not that far removed from embezzlement for the thrill of it. It is not simply thugs who are narcissistic and materialistic and babyish. It is all of us. Yet child welfare experts continue to treat those in their care as though children's behavior has no connection to the larger culture. And because it is individuals who are treated, not the larger culture, nothing will change in child welfare.

That being said, it might be possible to provide a better system than the one currently in place. For one thing, child welfare funding was massively cut during the Reagan years, and it has never been restored. One step toward improving the lot of American children in general would be to increase funding so that foster care, when needed, can be effective. There are some innovative programs out there that in fact bring foster parents into the troubled house rather than removing the children; those programs, of course, cost about three times what the current system does. However, these programs seem far more effective than what's going on now.

Another problem affecting the child welfare system right now is the inability to attract reasonable foster parents. Quite a few foster parents in many states adhere to a particularly rigid form of fundamentalist Christianity and require religious practice of the children they take in. This is simply appalling and needs to be stopped. Rather than providing a safe haven, one in which adults actually seem to be in charge, these kinds of foster parents substitute one form of infantilism for another. In addition, as the news media all too often tell us, a fair number of foster parents are themselves physically and/or sexually abusive themselves. This can become an especially difficult problem when children are placed in kin care. Social workers do not, or, more realistically, cannot, spend the time to recruit competent foster parents—there are simply not enough social workers on staff in any state child welfare department, and those who are there tend to be undereducated (those with M.S.Ws often go into administration). Again, it's clear that more money funneled into the system could help. Less money has hurt our children, and badly.

In a larger sense, though, what's really necessary is culture change. The psychotherapeutic metaphor simply cannot help the child welfare system. It has not worked, it does not work, and it will not work. What will work, instead, is a commitment on the part of child welfare workers to community organization, to political action, to building neighborhoods, to working on politicians to reform our economy and our culture. As long as we view children in foster care and abusive parents as isolated individuals rather than as part of a larger and very troubled culture, nothing is going to change. As long as we continue to celebrate the individual, and individual rights, rather than the greater good, children will continue to die.

I want my baby

Another aspect of all of this is the recent development of fertility treatments in lieu of adoption or indeed foster parentage. As women are waiting longer and longer to have children, the ability to conceive becomes more and more problematic. For poor folks, that's the end of the story—fertility treatments are not for the like of them. But for those with means, hundreds of thousands of dollars are spent to reproduce. The privileged, rather than adopting, choose to squander unimaginable amounts of money to obtain genetic facsimiles of themselves. In a society in which children are being beaten, sold on the streets for drugs, underfed or poorly fed, the wealthy monkey around with hormone shots, egg harvesting, in-vitro fertilization, and sperm counts. American culture truly has sunk to a new low when those unable to conceive can, on the one hand, reproduce after investing thousands and thousands and thousands of dollars, while, on the other hand, complain about their taxes. Conception through fertility specialists has to be one of the most immoral practices Americans have come up with in a long time.

Other societies are much more relaxed about such things. It is not uncommon for families to lend out some of their children to childless couples, for instance. The childless couples adopt a child; they gain an heir and someone to look after them in their old age. The child is allowed to continue to see his family but also must understand that the new parents are his parents. The biological parents are faced not only with one less child to feed, clothe, and educate but they also don't have to worry about that child, having placed him in a home they know. Now, granted, these kinds of arrangements work well in village-based societies where everyone either knows each other or are kin to each other. It is not completely ridiculous, though, to think that it could work in our culture if we could get rid of the notion that (1) we own our children and that (2) this confers upon us some kind of special privilege.

But the good of children rarely comes into play in decisions about fertility and adoption. For instance, perfectly awful parents who are horrible to their children still have rights—special hearings have to be held in order to terminate those rights. The concentration in American law on property rights rather than attending to larger issues of justice can be seen in fights by biological parents to keep their parental rights. The state must show overwhelming evidence that parents should lose their rights and that every other avenue has been explored. But why? Why is this such a big deal?

Again, in many societies, parents are far less focused on their children. In part because of high infant mortality rates, the sense of sentimentality Americans attach to children simply isn't there. Women get pregnant and might deliver safely and, if lucky, they will see most, though not all, of their children get to adulthood. While child death is difficult, it is not the trauma in most parts of the world that it is in the United States. Here in the United States, because our infant mortality rate is so low (though it is not the lowest rate in the world, in part due to our incredibly expensive and wasteful medical services delivery system; see Davis 2008), we tend to believe that children are amazing, unique, wonderful creatures who must be treasured and cherished and whose loss is absolutely devastating. That's if they belong to us, if they are our offspring.

This is an attitude borne of luxury. Most folks in the world cannot take this stance; they can't afford to. Death is a part of many people's lives, except in the United States. But just as we believe that we have a right to all manner of material items, we think we have a right to reproduce. Hogwash. There are moral ways to reproduce, and immoral ways. Abandoning already existing children to spend huge amounts of money because you have a right to spend your money any way you want is simply appalling behavior. Insisting that all fetuses must be born regardless of circumstance is similarly appalling, and declaring a fetus to be an actual baby is absurd, something also borne of luxury. There is nothing magical about reproduction.

Though it's silly to go as far as some geneticists to say that a baby is just a gene's way of copying itself, it is accurate to say that Americans' focus on begetting their own children, and ignoring those children already on the planet, is an unconscionable position.

Babies R Us

We remain in a furor as well about babies in other ways. Our society, for instance, particularly its mouths on the Right, argue about the "sanctity of life" and wish to stop all abortions. They sentimentalize children, though they do not wish to pay for them if the children are not "theirs," particularly (it seems) if the money is going to those of historically oppressed populations. On the Left, liberals somewhat timorously proclaim that abortion should be "safe, rare, and legal." Both positions come from an appallingly and unconsciously privileged set of assumptions.

Death, and child death in particular, is an unusual enough occurrence in the United States that it is seen as a tragedy; this heightens the anti-choice emotion, I think, since children really don't die here very much. Anti-abortion tirades do not occur in societies where children die regularly. Death of children is seen as regular and normal; why on earth would anyone get so upset about something that isn't even alive yet (according to them)? I am not saying that we should adopt that particular stance (though our abandonment of poor children through "welfare reform" is appallingly immoral). But the anti-choice stance is one of U.S. privilege and a relatively low infant mortality rate.

For instance, a female fetus (referred to almost exclusively by the media as a "baby girl," as a quick Google search reveals), Amillia Taylor, was saved at twenty-one weeks in October 2006 (Block 2007). She has had brain hemorrhaging, respiratory issues, and other significant medical problems. The fetus should have miscarried as was clearly needed. Instead, doctors and parents insisted on "saving" this "miracle" baby. For what? A life of developmental delays, costing us, either as taxpayers or insurance customers, hundreds of thousands, if not millions, of dollars (it should be noted that one of her doctors said that, had he known that the fetus was only almost twenty-two weeks, he might not have intervened in the miscarriage [*USA Today* 2007]). For a fetus that was trying to die. Just because we *can* do something (like make this fetus survive) doesn't mean we *should* do something.

This is a major question in medical ethics these days. Who decides how we're going to pay for what? Do we dedicate millions and millions and millions and millions of dollars for premature fetuses that will never live normal or even minimally useful lives? Do we put that money toward the end of life, extending the lives of our parents and grandparents? This assumes, of course, a zero-sum game of fixed financial resources.

The pro-life movement has its collective head in the sand, sentimentalizing cute little babies but being unwilling to make the very, very hard choices about our collective responsibility for the actual living, breathing, walking around human beings. Rather than representing God's view, as the anti-abortionists all too often say they do, the anti-choice movement hypocritically abandons children while insisting that all pregnant women must carry every child to full term. The invocation of various religious beliefs, by the way, in the discussion is not relevant. No religious law has any place in this country. This is not a theocracy.

In short, though on the face of it anti-abortionists argue that they are trying to save children, in the end all they do is insist on imposing suffering on women. They are not to be tolerated. Is this stance toward abortion unnecessarily cruel? Maybe. But the anti-choice movement advocates cruel consequences on American women. The pro-choice outrage is justified, calling pro-lifers on their hypocrisy is justified, and those of us on the Left had better become prepared to lose our civility. It is the basic decency of this nation that is at stake.

Not only is abortion a hot-ticket item. Daycare remains a matter of controversy. On the Right, the preachers claim that a woman's desire to be among adults, rather than children, to be unnatural. On the Left, the pundits claim that all women deserve a fulfilling career and great kids as well. Both sides make assumptions about daycare's role in all of this. It is a weird, postmodern, specifically American idea that mothers should be fascinated with their children and that children should consume all of the parents' time (and really we mean the mother's). Only in a country as wealthy and self-indulgent as ours would we think that it's somehow immoral to allow others to care for your children. The big difference, of course, is that instead of having people familiar to the children looking after them in the neighborhood, kids now have to travel to childcare "professionals." That in itself is bizarre from a cross-cultural perspective, but it's how we've set it up in the United States. It's been this way since after World War II and everyone decided married couples must live in their own houses away from their families.

This created a certain kind of family environment, with significant emotional enmeshment. The parents of Boomers seemed, for the most part, to feel somewhat liberated by moving out of the city and away from the extended family; it was something of a rite of passage of adulthood to buy the home in the suburbs, take on the mortgage, and go about setting up the Cleaver household. There remained, however, a strong sense of privacy for most Boomer parents. There was an adult world, and a childish sphere. Adults did not find the childish world all that fascinating.

It has to be noted, of course, that adults didn't find the adult world all that beguiling, either, particularly in the 1950s. As Stephanie Coontz has outlined very well in her social history of post–World War II families (Coontz 1992), there were significant pressures on both men and women to act in rather rigid ways, and to adhere to a relatively monolithic child-rearing and marital structure. Demands for conformity were strong, and the cultural script at that point was not particularly flexible. The script called for somewhat distant parenting, in different ways, from fathers and mothers, and a clearly subservient role for women, which led, as Friedan pointed out in *The Feminine Mystique* (1974 [1963]), to serious problems with alcohol and tranquilizer overuse. The parents of Boomers, then, were not always available to their children. Children's activities consisted, during the day anyway, of interactions largely with other children. While there were adult eyes on children in many parts of the country, those eyes were focused only occasionally on children and only once in a while on their own children. Adults had better things to do with their time, most of the time, than hang out with children. Again, children simply were not that interesting to adults.

Contrast that with parents today. It's close to heresy to say that you just don't find your children that fascinating. Parents are told, today, that they must be involved in all aspects of their children's lives. It's gotten to such a ridiculous extreme that parents are actively involved in their adult children's work progress. For instance, Lisa Belkin tells us (2007) that there are increasing reports that parents are writing their adult children's resumes, that parents are insisting on being part of salary negotiations, and that parents demand to know why their children were not hired (Belkin 2007). Certainly these seem to be the outliers but it is absolutely the case that parents are very involved with their children (but, apparently, with no one else's). Young people don't seem to mind it, either.

Parents—Boomer parents and beyond—are deeply involved in every aspect of their children's lives. They are fascinated, it appears, with everything from bowel movements to sex, from birth to whenever their children stop telling them things. Parents are (as noted elsewhere) insistent on being friends with their children. They don't seem to be want to be parents but they do want to be friends. Parents create a sense, I think, that there are no boundaries between the child and the parent, that there is little that is secret, that there is no authority, or, rather, that the child is the authority on everything. This cannot be good.

This leads, in my view, to infantilized children who have no sense of emotional boundaries or appropriateness of behavior. As I argued in chapter 2, our child-rearing techniques have produced profoundly narcissistic children. Certainly there is a bit of "when I was your age I walked uphill to school both ways in the blinding snow" mentality when we look at children today, and thus it ever was. At the same time, there seems to be a sea change in children's self-assessments. Jean Twenge, a psychologist (amazingly enough!) at San Diego State University, argues that young people in the twenty-first century have a strong sense of unhealthful narcissism:

> Today's college students are more narcissistic and self-centered than their predecessors, according to a new study by five psychologists who worry that the trend could be harmful to personal relationships and American society. "We need to stop endlessly repeating, 'You're special' and having children repeat that back," said the study's lead author, Professor Jean Twenge of San Diego State University. "Kids are self-centered enough already." (Associated Press 2007)

We do see young people today plagiarizing more (as noted in chapter 5), for instance, and parents trying every trick in the book to remove all consequences for poor behavior. Parents seem to regard their children as immune from any result that may come from misbehaving. After all, you shouldn't judge your friends—should you? No, that judgment is invoked only on people you don't like—like poor children, or children in the care of the state, or the children of gay men and lesbians.

Unnatural parents

American culture becomes even more disturbing in discussions of adoption by gay men and lesbians. As I write, gay men and lesbians are allowed to marry only in Massachusetts, and, for the moment anyway, in California, but not in the rest of the United States, although some are allowed to adopt (single women also are allowed to adopt, though in most states single men cannot). However, the reactionary backlash against such arrangements by no less than the late John Paul II, as well as his far more conservative successor Benedict XVI—both of whom continue to insist that homosexuals should never be allowed to marry (Rocca 2007), that homosexual behavior is abhorrent, and that homosexuals should never be allowed to rear children—is relatively strong. Other fundamentalists make a similar argument: the purpose of marriage, as ordained by their God, is to procreate. Homosexuals cannot procreate "naturally" and therefore have no right to demand the right to child-rearing or marriage.

There are fatal flaws, of course, in this discussion. Those who use fertility drugs therefore are sinful, since they cannot procreate without technological help and therefore should not be married even if heterosexual (to be fair, John Paul II and the Catholic Church in general had also condemned those activities). Those who do not procreate at all, whether for medical or other reasons, but are heterosexual and married, are not really married and are sinful. When we add in homosexuals who want to marry or to rear children, we begin looking at a large minority of the American population, under this skewed logic, that is sinful. It's not clear, however, that the wish by a homosexual to rear a child, or even simply for anyone, gay or straight, to have non-procreative sex, is evil.

Homosexuals are also often accused of evil intentions in rearing children. The thought apparently is that homosexuals will teach their children to be homosexual, which is apparently a bad thing. However, this notion can be removed immediately: sexuality does not seem to be solely a learned behavior, since homosexuals grew up largely in heterosexual families and yet they did not learn how to be heterosexual (Stacy 1996: 105–144). Though the science at this writing remains very unclear, it appears that sexual orientation in fact is partly genetic. We can see this from a simple cross-cultural examination. In many, though by no means all, societies, there is an acknowledgment that a certain portion of the population will prefer same-sex sexual relationships. Generally speaking and on average, somewhere in the area of 5% of any given population will contain men and women who are aroused largely by members of their own gender. Given this, it appears actually that homosexuality is one form of sexuality that humans have devised, through the process of evolution, and is therefore as "natural" as heterosexuality. If such behaviors exist cross-culturally, it's fair to say that it is part of the human genome at least for some humans.

Indeed, Kinsey and Masters and Johnson discovered nearly fifty years ago that human sexuality is remarkably flexible. Few humans are either solely homosexual or solely heterosexual. Most of us fall somewhere in between, with some of us able to be aroused by either sex, some of us less able to be aroused by our same sex, and some of us more able to be aroused by our same sex. Sexuality then is not carved in stone but is malleable, as is so much of human behavior. Granted, some societies will discourage same-sex sexuality, and others will not mind it so much for a variety of reasons, just as some societies encourage emotionality and individuality and others promote group cohesion and extended families.

All of this means that homosexual parents are neither more nor less likely to teach children to be homosexual. Particularly in the case of adoption, homosexual parents will be dealing in part with their children's genetic makeup, in part with the larger culture, and in part with their own family dynamics. There simply is no legitimate reason to deny gay men and lesbians the ability to rear children.

Now, some would argue that the children of homosexuals might be teased, and that would be harmful to the children. This is a specious argument as well. That is not the problem of the parents and the children but rather of those doing the teasing. Just as we do not forbid African Americans to marry European Americans and then to reproduce, on the grounds that children of mixed ethnic heritage might be teased, we cannot forbid same-sex marriage and child-rearing. It simply is immoral, illogical, and unwise to do so.

Such a scheme is immoral since it does little to advance the greater good of American society. Discriminatory practices against marriage and family creation, solely on the basis of religion and half-baked pseudo-scientific theories, reminds the thoughtful American of earlier prohibitions against intermarriage between various ethnic groups or various religious groups. The United States should be better than that by now.

Prohibitions against homosexual marriage and family creation are illogical since they are based on absolutely no solid or credible scientific information. Those who proclaim that children of homosexual unions will be harmed in some amorphous way are wrong. There is no evidence to support their points. Use of the Bible and idiosyncratic interpretations of its meaning, if any, is not a legitimate course of setting social policy. Christians cannot agree on the importance of the Bible in constructing societies; one, rather oddball view of it cannot be a foundation for good social policy. Furthermore, not everyone in the United States is Christian in any recognizable way. Why should a vocal minority—those who make up fundamentalist Christianity—determine the behaviors and social policies affecting the rest of us? While the United States was originally colonized by Englishmen and women with some unusual views (to say the least), those perspectives were not much part of the United States envisioned by Jefferson, Franklin, Washington, and their colleagues 150 years later. The United States has never been a "Christian" country, and it has never been led by "Christian" values narrowly defined by fundamentalists today. Therefore, it is illogical to argue that homosexual marriage and child-rearing is somehow un-American.

Finally, the denial of marriage and family life to homosexuals is unwise. The civil rights movements of the 1960s changed American society in basic ways—some good, some bad. However, we did finally realize that discrimination against entire groups of people on the basis of a shaky religious belief or simply to keep hold of what the elite had is a poor idea. Groups as well as individuals in the United States have rights, painstakingly pulled out of those in power grudgingly at best. Homosexuals are among those groups claiming important rights. To ignore those claims is unwise, especially since homosexuality is spread throughout the population and not just limited to one ethnic group or social class. We will regret it if we continue to retreat to a position of ignoring clear evidence.

Homosexuals rearing children make no more of a hash of it than any other parents. They make the same mistakes outlined in this book. There are homosexual parents who are good parents; there are those who are bad. But they are no more good or bad than any other parent in the United States.

Family values?

We've come a long way from child welfare systems to homosexual parents. In all of this, however, what can be seen is that child welfare experts seem unable to comprehend a larger world beyond their rather limited worldviews. The child welfare system in the United States is marred by an ignorant ethnocentrism and, oftentimes, by a frightening religiosity. Both tendencies need to be squelched. From poorly recruited and trained foster parents to judgments about adoption, the child welfare system and its workers needs significant maturing and expansion if we truly are to have family values.

Chapter 7
Still Crazy after All These Years

It's probably not an exaggeration to say that a new "mental illness" is defined every month or so. From Post-traumatic Stress Disorder (PTSD) to Relationship Dysfunction, Americans are diagnosed right and left as having serious emotional disorders. Those of us who deny that we're sick are in denial and need a good helping of major psychotherapy to help us acknowledge our problems. *The Diagnostic and Statistical Manual IV* (DSM IV) of the American Psychiatric Association continues to be revised, allegedly based on "scientific" evidence that is in no way scientific but still is quite convenient for therapists. Even those psychologists and social workers who are less than convinced that DSM IV is all that useful bristle at the notion that there may be little to no provable mental illness.

But notice that "little to no." What is clear, from cross-cultural evidence, is that there appear to be perhaps three identifiable mental illnesses that are true illnesses—that is, that have a clear biogenetic component. Those are schizophrenia, bipolar disorder, and, perhaps (only perhaps) major depression. The rest of the maladies listed in DSM IV are cultural constructions, useful (it appears) categories with which to judge behavior. Anorexia, for instance, is quite clearly a culture-bound syndrome—it only is exhibited in North America and, to a lesser degree, some Western European countries. Voluntarily starving oneself is not often a prized behavior in most societies. It is not a mental illness, in that there is absolutely no evidence that it has a biogenetic basis. Yet anorexia, like just about everything else in DSM IV, is treated as though it is a medical rather than cultural condition.

The psychotherapeutic metaphor for diagnosis

Why do Americans have the impulse to believe that their behaviors are caused by a physical illness rather than by themselves or those around them? Once again, the psychotherapeutic metaphor provides the answer. It is far easier, and far less expensive, to see—for instance—an anorexic girl with body image problems in long-term therapy than it is to change a set of cultural values that promote unrealistic expectations for body shape and size. And only in a land of plenty would this be an issue. Children who starve themselves by choice can do so only in a society where there is food to refuse. As with so many other issues, American dominant culture promotes, on the one hand, a puritanical emphasis on denial of bodily pleasure—more specifically, eating—with, more recently, a concern with Big Macs and obesity. Both sets of behaviors, though, are filtered through the lens of the psychotherapeutic metaphor.

Anorexia and obesity in young people are lately discussed as medical illnesses, caused by a flawed interiority rather than a flawed culture. Anorexics are told by psychotherapists, physicians, the media, and the culture at large that thin is good so thinner must be better. Obese children, on the other hand, are marketed to by large corporations and are provided for by weary parents (Linn 2005: 95–104). Both conditions, though, are construed as individual problems rather than cultural ones. We seem to refuse to see that, again, only in a society that has little to worry about day to day, at least in terms of being able to obtain food, that we can become so obsessed with it. These are problems that emerge from an individualistic, narcissistic culture rather than some kind of broken internal process. American culture encourages extreme behaviors.

And the only way we can then explain aberrations is through the psychotherapeutic metaphor. We do not criticize or try to alter the subsidized capitalistic system in which we live, the system that provides images to sell to children (and adults) in attempts to persuade Americans to either be a size 2 or to consume a Whopper. American parents do not often stop children from unhealthful behaviors; instead, they value their children's rights to be thin or to be fat as they work very hard to ensure that their children's self-esteem is not damaged. Anorexia and obesity are understood not as selfish, self-centered, immoral behaviors but instead as resulting from poor self-images. Anorexia and obesity are not seen as behaviors encouraged by a larger selfish, self-centered culture but as individual problems, resolvable, perhaps, through psychotherapy or summer camps. We are not to judge either those engaged in these behaviors or the larger culture fomenting them.

Anorexia as culture-bound

Most analysts note, but hardly anyone remarks on, the fact that anorexia is a set of behaviors that is associated with young, *middle- to upper-middle-class* North American European American women (Bordo 1993; Wolf 1994; Way 1995). The fact that anorectics are women is grist for the analytic mill, and the fact that they are adolescents often also is important. Sometimes their ethnicity is analyzed (Gremillion 2003; Thompson 1994). But class position is merely noted rather than discussed. I suggest that our understanding of anorexia must be understood not only in traditionally feminist frameworks—that of the oppressive nature of the continuing patriarchy, demanding slenderness, control, and self-sacrifice—but it must also be understood in a larger, global context. We need to see anorexia as a culture-bound syndrome, one with real young women who suffer, to be sure, but one that can only occur in a highly privileged population. Just as a bow to bona fides, I should note that I practiced family therapy in the Chicago area in the 1980s, and part of my clientele included eating-disordered families. I later took a Ph.D. in psychological anthropology. My discussion, however, is largely analytical and theoretical rather than aimed at treatment issues.

Culture-bound syndromes

Essentially, culture-bound syndromes are troublesome patterns of behavior that are specific to and congruent with a particular culture. That is, these patterns of behavior are understood within a set of cultural understandings most often as unusual and as difficult, as devalued deviance. Here in the United States, we tend to call those patterns of devalued deviance "mental illness" and we lately treat such behaviors as grounded in biological or genetic malfunction—not social or cultural dysfunction—that can be managed through, most often, chemical management using pharmaceuticals in individuals rather than working through larger groups. We call upon the *Diagnostic and Statistical Manual*, the DSM, compiled and published by the American Psychiatric Association, to scientistically classify difficult or troublesome behaviors.

In most other societies, however, culture-bound syndromes are understood by those afflicted and by those observing the affliction in a society as emerging from social and cultural conditions that require social and cultural cures. Certainly it is an individual person who is troubled, but the cause of the trouble is often socially based—angry ancestor spirits, for instance, may cause suffering in an innocent victim for the transgressions of a kinsperson. If one of your kin has offended the spirits, and it often is not clear which kinsperson has done this, all your kin must be involved in propitiating the angry spirit. It is not the individual sufferer's burden alone. In the majority of the world's societies, dysfunctional behavior is interpreted as caused, and cured, by a larger set of beings than just the individual (Throop 1991).

Contrast that with the West, and more specifically with North America. Our reliance in this country in particular on DSM IV and various psychotropic and other psychiatric drugs places the locus of suffering squarely on the individual. The problem here is that almost all of the DSM categories have little basis in reliable and verifiable data (Kutchins and Kirk 1997). Only some schizophrenias, bipolar disorder, and major depression seem have clearly demonstrable biogenetic bases (though even there we cannot aver that biology is the only cause for these difficulties, only that a certain biogenetic platform must be in place) (Murphy 1976; Throop 1992). The rest of the "diseases" in this compendium are actually culture-bound syndromes, including things such as Attention Deficit-Hyperactivity Disorder (ADHD), various sexual dysfunctions, personality disorders, and anxiety disorders.

So too is anorexia conceptualized by the psychotherapeutic community and indeed by the dominant culture, far too influenced by this folk metaphor.

Anorexia: Culture- and class-bound syndrome

So what is anorexia, at least to the dominant culture of the United States? According to the DSM IV, anorexia is

> [r]efusal to maintain body weight at or above a minimally normal weight for age and height (e.g., weight loss leading to maintenance of body weight less than 85% of that expected or failure to make expected weight gain during period of growth, leading to body weight less than 85% of that expected). Intense fear of gaining weight or becoming fat, even though underweight. Disturbance in the way in which one's body weight or shape is experience, undue influence of body weight or shape on self-evaluation, or denial of the seriousness of the current low body weight. In post-menarchal females, amenorrhea, i.e., the absence of at least three consecutive cylces. (A woman is considered to have amenorrhea if her periods occur only following hormone, e.g., estrogen, administration.) Specify type: Restricting type: During the current episode of anorexia nervosa, the person has

> not regularly engaged in binge-eating or purging behavior (i.e., self-induced vomiting or the misuse of laxatives, diuretics, or enemas).
> Binge-Eating/Purging type: during the current episode of anorexia nervosa, the person has regularly engaged in binge-eating or purging behavior (i.e., self-induced vomiting or the misuse of laxatives, diuretics, or enemas). (Cleveland Clinic 2004)

Sounds very scientific, doesn't it? DSM III and IV have been heralded by those accepting this compendium of troublesome behaviors as being both nicely descriptive in terms of symptomology (thereby easing diagnosis) and as constituting both clear reliability and validity in terms of symptomology. By calling these difficult behaviors "illnesses" and "diseases," we lose the cultural basis undergirding these actions.

That is the case, of course, with anorexia. We do know that, according to the National Institute of Mental Health, somewhere between .5% and 3.7% of young women will be understood as anorectic at some point in their lives (http://www.nimh.nih.gov/publicat/eatingdisorders.cfm). We also know that physicians and those embedded within the psychotherapeutic community continue to insist that this is a real disease, arguing that there are genetic, biochemical, and neurological bases to this "illness" (ibid.; Park 2004). Granted, some of these researchers will pay lip service to what the psychotherapeutic community calls "environment," but the focus of treatment is on the individual young woman, and sometimes, discouragingly, her mother. There are no medical or psychotherapeutic movements of which I am aware that call for cultural change, just individual change, through drug and talk therapy. The neglect of culture in the treatment of this very dangerous set of behaviors is difficult to comprehend.

Anorexia as cross-cultural

However, if anorexia *is* genetically, biochemically, or neurologically based, we should see it outside of the United States and Canada, in the same percentages. If, like schizophrenia, anorexia is a biologically based disease rather than a culture-bound syndrome, anorexia should appear worldwide. *Yet it does not.* A few psychologists have attempted to demonstrate that anorexia is not a culture-bound syndrome but is a "real" "mental illness" (Keel and Klump 2003), but their studies are flawed.

Keel and Klump, for instance, argue that their study shows conclusively that we see anorexia in parts of Africa, Asia, the Middle East, and Europe (2003: 756). But almost all of the studies upon which they relied for their meta-analysis do not provide the diagnostic criteria upon which anorexia was identified. The inexactitude of the methodology means we cannot rely on Keel and Klump's assertions.

Furthermore, Keel and Klump make some astounding claims. For instance, they argue that the sufferers of anorexia, or the members of the society—presumably non-Western—to which the sufferers belong, may offer explanations for anorectic behavior that "...may not represent the *true causes* of self-starvation" (Keel and Klump 2003: 754; emphasis added). In other words, there are "true causes" of anorexia out there, but only trained observers can see them, not those afflicted with the behavioral patterns nor nonafflicted societal members. Cultural explanations are, apparently, irrelevant to these researchers. Instead, they implicitly argue that DSM is somehow objective, culture-free, and ahistorical and that anorexia is universal.

I think it is not unreasonable to state, with no qualms, that anorexia is a culture-bound syndrome, limited to the wealthy West or to those societies heavily influenced by the West. All verifiable evidence points to this conclusion. So anorexia is culture-bound; now we need to examine claims that anorexia is also part of human history.

Historically bound

Indeed, one therapist has argued, to some misguided acclaim, that anorexia must be a part of our human evolutionary heritage (Guisinger 2003). Shan Guisinger, who apparently is a psychologist in private practice in Montana, asserts that anorexia had an adaptive advantage in our evolutionary past. Assuming that life for humans prior to the development of agriculture was nasty, brutish, and short, Guisinger seems to believe that our evolutionary environments meant constant food insecurity. Therefore, the suppression of appetite—this seemingly is how she understands anorexia for the purposes of her paper—had an adaptive advantage. If you're hungry yet you don't feel hungry, you'll survive to find that woolly mastodon another day.

The problem of course is that it is not at all clear that life prior to the development of agriculture 10,000 years ago was nasty, brutish, and short. Our African and Asian environments appear to have been relatively abundant, and it is likely that our European environments were not that difficult either (with the exception of a few pesky Ice Ages). Instead, it is after the development of domesticated plants and animals that famine, starvation, and malnutrition step in, as any anthropologist can tell you (that also, by the way, is likely to be when patriarchy was created; cf. McElvaine 2001).

So if anorexia is not an evolutionary strategy—and it is not—can we say at least that it is part of recorded human history? Certainly a number of scholars try to argue this. For instance, among others, anthropologist Rebecca Lester claims that self-starvation was a common theme in the lives of some medieval religious women (Lester 1995). She goes on to say, however, that while the behaviors of medieval female ascetics may look like current-day anorectics, those religious women cannot be placed in the same category as the anorectic of the twentieth century. Lester asserts that the ideation of medieval religious women had a motivation quite different from today's anorectics—the ascetic women were looking for a closer communion with God. Lester's analysis asserts as well that medieval religious ascetic women were also attempting to gain control over their bodies as their families were trying to determine their young women's futures (Lester 1995: 215). Lester concludes that behaviors that look like current-day anorexia in fact are culturally and historically bound, and that they are not comparable.

Other scholars are less exact in their analyses. Keel and Klump (2003), our psychologists discussed earlier, embark on an ambitious project to summarize the literature on "holy anorexia," the term coined by Bell (1985 as cited in Keel and Klump 2003: 752). They conclude that cases of self-starvation from medieval times through Freudian times are in fact anorexia as currently conceived and seem to ignore the anthropological and historical analyses demonstrating otherwise. They claim: "...across historical contexts women deliberately refuse to eat food that they require for sustenance" (Keel and Klump 2003: 254). That is, once again we see a refusal to understand the nuances of culture and history in this insistence that anorexia was, is, and (I suppose) evermore will be a mental illness. Keel and Klump are trying to show that anorexia has existed historically and cross-culturally (so too do Bynum 1997 and Brumberg 1997) in their attempt to demonstrate it is biogentic in nature just as schizophrenia is. They are incorrect.

Based firmly in class position

One thing that goes unnoted in the discussions of medieval female ascetics and those allegedly displaying anorectic symptoms cross-culturally is that almost all persons described come from Western privileged classes. While ethnicity and gender are often analyzed, social class rarely is. Why is this?

It could be argued that class issues rarely are discussed in U.S. culture in any substantive way. At least in our dominant culture, including the media but also to a large extent in the public primary and secondary schools, certainly there is little recognition that our society is a clearly unequal one, in which a very few own most of the resources and assets available. It appears that most of dominant culture does not recognize the real barriers placed in front of those who are not upper-middle-class European Americans. If someone is poor, it is because she is lazy. If someone hits another person, it is because he has anger issues. And, if someone is anorectic, it is because she has body image issues, or an addictive personality, or a dysfunctional family. Rarely in dominant culture is a larger discussion held about culture, history, or society, and in almost all issues the only solution is therapy (even for poverty!). This is an inadequate response.

Now, to be fair, anorexia *has* been considered in terms of culture, history, and society by feminist scholars, at least to some extent, as we've already noted. However, class issues have not been considered much by those exploring anorexia. One set of researchers attempted to show that anorexia in fact is not class-specific (Gard and Freeman 1996). Unfortunately, they not only continually mixed bulimia with anorexia but also—if you can believe this—asserted that homeless people are afflicted with eating disorders (Gard and Freeman 1996: 9)! They conclude that bulimia is not class-based nor based in any particular ethnicity (which seems to be true to some extent) and therefore neither is anorexia. Clearly, there are methodological problems here.

More promisingly, Helen Gremillion, in *Feeding Anorexia: Gender and Power at a Treatment Center* (2003: 156–192), analyzes class and ethnicity at length in her gripping study of an inpatient hospital dealing in part with eating-disordered girls. She argues, convincingly, that young women of color who enter with a diagnosis of anorexia but who do not conform to dominant culture are rediagnosed by the treatment center as "borderline" personality disorder. Gremillion asserts—again, I believe correctly—that the young women who do not follow the script provided by the hospital, who argue with it, are transferred to other wards. It is not coincidence that all young women of color are placed into these categories. Gremillion concludes by demonstrating that much of psychotherapy, particularly family therapy, is built on dominant cultural understandings to which the privileged European American classes aspire but which make little sense, intellectually, emotionally, culturally, or demographically, to nonprivileged young women. Gremillion's discussion of class and ethnic issues is about the best I've seen in the various analyses of anorexia that have appeared in the past twenty years or so, though it explores ethnicity far more than social class.

So how is it that anorexia became so class-based? How is it that it became so identified with European American women? And perhaps most importantly, how is it that anorexia became so medicalized or at least "expertized?"

The answer to all three questions lies, I think, in social class and privilege. Let's consider the "holy anorexics" some analysts claim are the same kinds of anorectics that we see today. Those medieval religious ascetics came from the privileged classes in Europe. It was impossible for a woman to enter a convent, or to devote her life to God, without strong family resources behind her. The idea that one could live a life of contemplation required others to do your share of work for you. Only the privileged could make such demands. Moreover, convents at the time required significant dowries before a girl could become a "bride of Christ." So if we accept that the "holy anorexics" were similar to anorectics today—and even if we don't—we can see that voluntary self-starvation has historical precedent embedded in class issues.

Second, we know that most anorexia today is identified with European American young women. Why? Because we also know that it is European Americans who hold the vast majority of wealth, assets, and resources in this country. Certainly it is only a small subset of European Americans, but few people of color command the kinds of power and wealth that this small subset of European Americans does. If you are poor, you are likely food-insecure. You will not willfully starve yourself, and in fact the data show that there are few volunteers for malnutrition and starvation among the poor and dispossessed of this country. It is only with privilege that the option for self-starvation appears. That is, only if you have enough, or too many, resources, can you refuse to partake.

Further, with privilege comes leisure time. We know this is true cross-culturally, and we know this is true historically. As societies become more complex, particularly with the advent of agriculture, great differences in wealth, and leisure time, become apparent. Those with privilege have the luxury of time to consider their lives beyond the next meal, the next day, or the next year. With food security can come self-reflection and dissatisfaction. No longer worried about the next meal, the privileged can, and do, focus their attention on their interiorities.

This, I think, is the heart of the matter. Anorectics, because they are privileged in this country, have the ability to focus on themselves to the point of death. Indeed, twenty-first century anorectics can be distinguished from medieval ascetic women in a further important way. Medieval self-starving women framed their voluntary starvation, and their suffering, in a context of ecstatic religious experience, embedding their behaviors in a deep sense of larger purpose. Twenty-first-century American anorectics seem to be focused solely on self, with no larger moral meaning to their behaviors.

And American dominant culture encourages such self-exploration, such narcissism. By creating a culture of psychotherapy, in which emotions are all worthy of exploration, experience and expression, we all play a part in the creation and maintenance of anorexia. Rather than embedding our understandings of behavior in a clear set of ideals based on social justice, we abet anorexia by asserting that each person is entitled to her feelings and to act on those feelings. We need to understand the feelings—of self-hatred, of negative body image, of oppression—in order to help the sufferer get past them. Nowhere may we ask for some responsibility from the sufferers—at least, we must not judge the suffering privileged.

I have a hard time with this. The latest numbers from the World Health Organization (WHO) tell us that every year 792 million people across the globe—largely from Asia but also from Africa and the Americas—are at high risk for food insecurity (www. who. org). Involuntary starvation seems to me to be a much more pressing problem, and one to which our resources ought to be going, rather than focusing on the suffering of a few privileged westerners. At the least, we need to be embedding larger issues within individual psychotherapy. But more on that soon.

What cannot be denied is that there are young women in the United States who are suffering greatly for a variety of reasons, even if some of those reasons may seem to be located outside our understandings of global social justice. Our treatment of anorexia seems to only compound the problem, at least according to Helen Gremillion (2003). Gremillion, mentioned above, describes an inpatient treatment unit for anorexia that mouths autonomy and independence for its patients but in fact enforces strict regimens of calorie counting, limited exercise, and constant staff surveillance of the young women on the ward. There also is a clear description of the staff members understanding themselves as better parents than the young women's parents.

Through an assertion that professionals can parent children better than those pesky amateurs, actual parents, anorexia "experts" tend to remove parents from any treatment picture. Those experts then control when the actual parents can see their children, and the experts control how parents may communicate with children. If parents do not accept the dominant culture's psychotherapeutic metaphor, they are not allowed access to their children. I find this state of affairs disturbing. An insistence on one, and only one, right way to parent is difficult to accept, especially when this parenting method, solidly middle class, demands an emphasis on rights over obligations. Again, a discussion of the psychotherapeutic metaphor will wait for a bit.

Still, anorectics are treated as patients, rather than culturally embedded sufferers. They are given drugs and individual therapy and their emotions are attended to, both by themselves and by the staff of the psychotherapeutic environments in which they are housed. The cause of the problem is individual in nature; the treatment is individual in nature as well. There are a myriad of reasons for such an individual focus, as has been argued throughout this book. However, as the treatment of anorectics has gone through time—I hesitate to say "progressed"—the locus of treatment has become smaller and smaller. Those of us who were therapists to eating disordered families started out with a focus on the family, not really realizing that the family remains too small a treatment unit (see Epstein 1997: 185–195). But anymore even families are removed from treatment, and anorexia is understood today as an individual medical, psychopathological problem that needs the attention of physicians, psychiatrists, psychologists, nurses, social workers, and counselors. There is significant research being conducted looking at drugs specifically aimed at anorectics; there are claims that anorexia is a genetically based disease rather than a culture-bound syndrome; and so we go on.

The psychotherapeutic metaphor

So here we are. By allowing the privileged to explore, experience, and express their feelings, our society has helped to create and maintain anorexia. By encouraging children to "be themselves," to "express themselves," we have created some pretty self-involved children. *Time Magazine* reported a few years back that many parents have decided it is not their responsibility to teach their children how to act right and are instead turning to etiquette schools; one psychologist, apparently approving of these schools, is paraphrased as saying that "youngsters are inclined to regard teachers rather than parents as authority figures on subjects like proper behavior" (Gill and Sanders 2004: 55). In other words, we now have constructed parents as knowing hardly anything. This is distressing: how can parents understand themselves as *not knowing* about "proper behavior"?

Anorexia is tied up in this precisely because of what could be seen as the abdication of parents in terms of child-rearing. While some parents try to teach their children to be aware of the needs of others before attending to their own, others find their children's behavior wonderfully expressive and delightfully unique—even as those children throw tantrums or break the belongings of others. Now, parents today do have tremendous pressure on them—too many work hours, not enough pay, significant marketing and media influences on children and on adults, rampant consumerism, and overall major stress.

It's my view, though, that some of this is in part self-imposed. As Paul Campos points out in *The Obesity Myth: Why America's Obsession with Weight is Hazardous to Your Health* (2004), the middle and upper classes, at least, have supersized everything—homes, cars, kitchens, televisions, interiority, you name it (everything but themselves). All of this costs money, or at the least, credit cards. I am not sure why we have allowed this state of affairs to exist, since I certainly do not see children, or adults, remarkably happier today than they were when I was a child. Instead, I see many children suffering from afflictions of interiority, from paying too much attention to themselves and not enough to others, and I include anorexia in that statement. And psychotherapy encourages this.

Psychotherapy as morally and culturally bound

As I asserted earlier, psychotherapy now provides the primary metaphor for our dominant culture, at least for the privileged (the nonprivileged continue to be arrested, shot, jailed, or murdered for behaviors that the privileged receive therapy for). Rather than being shamed or punished for what could been as horrible errors, the privileged are shown how to explore their feelings even further than our child-rearing practices already do. Psychotherapy tells you that you are responsible only for your own interiority and your own feelings. You do not cause anyone else's pain, suffering, or feelings. Those belong to her, not to you. Do not take responsibility for anyone else; that's codependency. Don't put anyone ahead of yourself; that's self-defeating personality disorder.

Well, nonsense. Human beings are social animals. We evolved taking responsibility for those in our group; we evolved helping others. We act in concert with others; we do in fact cause other people pain, suffering, and feelings. We are interactional, social animals! We owe others something, especially when we're privileged, but all the time for everyone. We owe each other courtesy. We owe each other the right to be healthy. We owe each other quite a bit for our privileges. But our culture of capitalism, shaped by the psychotherapeutic metaphor, prohibits statements of responsibility, of obligation. Despite the fact that most other cultures are very clear that rights are always tempered, and often superceded, by obligations, we continue to believe that we are rugged individuals, connected to no one and to nothing that we haven't made ourselves.

And this again is where anorexia comes in. By insisting that anorexia is *not* based in social class (or ethnicity, for that matter), by insisting that it is not culturally bound, by insisting that it is a medical and not a cultural and social issue, we are rewarding privilege, reifying a set of cultural understandings privileging emotion over behavior and rights over obligations. Young women die because of this, and because of our continual insistence that emotions and behaviors shouldn't be judged—at least the emotions and behaviors of the privileged.

Including the moral in psychotherapy and in our understanding of human behavior, at least in the United States

Yet we *do* make judgments. We believe that emotional expression is good—that is a value statement. We believe that we should not judge but understand others—that is a value statement. We believe that shaming is bad—that is a value statement. We tend to think that only the religious Right embeds their discourse in morality. But those on the Left and on the Right make clear moral statements all the time. The problem is that some on the Left—usually those more conservative than me—argue that just about all behaviors are acceptable and come from "natural" emotions. But this reification is incorrect: emotions are *not* natural, they do not stand alone, but instead are culturally constructed. There is no way to separate the two. Emotions do not necessarily lead inevitably to behaviors, yet we believe they do (we call people who do not act on their emotions "repressed").

If we were to embed psychotherapy in a larger moral context, in a context of obligation rather than one based solely in rights, I believe anorectics could be shown a new kind of agency. If we can truly understand the privilege that comes from living in the United States, perhaps anorectics can abandon the contempt they demonstrate—granted, probably unthinkingly—for those who are truly and involuntarily starving across the world. Perhaps by having a truly global politics, our parochial but privileged American behaviors, including anorexia, can be eliminated as we understand ourselves in true cross-cultural context. That is, we need to understand that what we think, as Americans, to be true, right, and natural is no more true, right, and natural than any other cultural belief system. Psychotherapy is embedded within a cultural context, as is DSM, the "science" of psychology, and everything else we do.

If we can understand that culture truly is something that is largely created, rather than a set of "natural" behavior, we can provide change, agency, and possibilities not only for the young women, the anorectics who suffer in the United States, but for all who are starving.

Is there a doctor in the house?

Some of this can be traced, perhaps, to a larger discussion sometimes occurring in psychotherapeutic, anthropological, sociological, and other academic programs. A well-known truism is that much of American (and, more generally, Western) behavior is explained through the invocation of the medical model—that is, that behavior is internally motivated and caused. In the case of a cold virus, for instance, it's well documented that at least some of the external, behavioral symptoms—sneezing, coughing, sniffing heavily—are the result of the body's immune system responding to an invasion of viral microbes. A good understanding of the common cold requires a medical model—an explanation based on physiological, internal factors that lead to the experience of uncomfortable symptoms. Although at last count there are over 200 rhinoviruses documented, the cold virus acts in pretty much the same way in the right conditions. The medical model works here, and little of a sociocultural explanation really is necessary to understand the cold virus.

However, when we move from a relatively simply physiological reaction to an invading virus to invoking the same model to understand complex human behaviors, such as refusing to eat, the medical model falls woefully short (Simons and Hughes 1985). Yet we continue as a society to attempt to explain human actions in simple medical and physiological terms. DSM IV, for instance, is a compendium of hundreds of what are called mental illnesses—in other words, DSM and its adherents conceive of behavioral problems and human suffering as akin to physical illness (Kutchins and Kirk 1997). Those who contribute to DSM—largely psychiatrists and psychologists—seem to believe, in large part, that much of troublesome human behavior has at its basis biological factors. At the same time, DSM and its users acknowledge that those suffering from mental illness rarely can be cured; symptoms can be eased through the use of psychopharmacological drugs, but the underlying disease will never go away.

This is all a bit odd, since there are few predictive tests for any kind of mental illness (though there are of course for some physical illnesses, particularly various cancers). Although it is clear that schizophrenia, for instance, has a biogenetic base, there are no biological tests at present that can be performed that will accurately predict whether a particular person has the genetic and biological makeup to "contract" the "disease." In addition, the drugs prescribed for various types of schizophrenia seem to be effective in only about 30% of the cases (Throop 1992). In addition, one fact for the argument that schizophrenia is truly a disease rather than a culture-bound syndrome is that the brains and blood chemistry of some—though not all, by any means—schizophrenics is different than non-schizophrenics. These differences emerge in those who have been displaying schizophrenic behavior for a long time (indeed, the brain evidence comes largely from autopsies). No information has been taken on people who might start displaying schizophrenic symptoms since, as noted before, it is impossible to predict.

There is more than physiology going on here, but these days the treatment of choice is almost solely drugs. Furthermore, those involved with persons diagnosed as schizophrenic seem unable to challenge the dominant paradigm; I suspect they have enough on their plates as they try to help these seriously disturbed people act right and take their meds. But the drugs don't work. Now, some of the explanations for that harbor on explanations for why religious ritual doesn't work: it's not that the assumption—schizophrenia is biologically based—is wrong, it's that it was the wrong drug, or the person displaying schizophrenic symptoms took the drugs wrong, or didn't take enough. Just as believers never question the basic assumption—God exists and answers prayers—the mental health professions do not question whether schizophrenia might be more than a physical disease.

This is not to say, by the way, that there are no genetic or biological factors involved in schizophrenia (Fabrega 2002). Medical research has proven conclusively that genetic background is important: those with at least one schizophrenic parent or full sibling have a higher likelihood of displaying similar symptoms, even if they were not raised with their biological families (Throop 1992). That's not insignificant. It's also clear that the brain, a very flexible organ, adjusts to input received; this is what is called the plasticity of the human brain. If a person acts weird and is diagnosed as schizophrenic, in the classic self-fulfilling prophecy, that person learns how to act schizophrenic, taking in information and cultural expectations about how to act correctly in her role. Schizophrenics, like alcoholics, are told that they will never get well, although they are assured that, with the right medication, their symptoms may abate. The brain adapts to what is received and adjusts its pathways to allow for psychotic breaks and odd behavior.

It would be fascinating to experiment with a different model. What would happen, for instance, if a person experiencing random psychotic thoughts was told that he had caught the behavioral equivalent of pneumonia, requiring the solicitous care of family and friends? A short-term course of drug therapy to ameliorate the worst symptoms, a significant amount of bed rest, moderate exercise as the sufferer begins to feel better, the involvement of family and friends in all treatment would be prescribed. Indeed, this is what is done in some innovative Indian programs in Mumbai, Chennai, New Delhi, and other Indian cities (Throop 1992). There are no reported further psychotic episodes, after an entire family is hospitalized along with the sufferer. What would happen if the American psychiatric establishment insisted on full involvement by all family members of a schizophrenic?

There would be a rebellion, that's what would happen. Although for a brief moment in research on schizophrenia there were glimmerings of understanding behavior from at least a family systems point of view (Wynne, Haley, Jackson, and others, for instance) that has all been abandoned as the medical model has been fully embraced. Family members are not responsible for the behaviors of their "ill" relative; it is the disease causing the psychosis, not the larger system. Instead of family therapy including the schizophrenic member, those with suffering relatives are provided with family education. They are taught about the medical nature of this disease and about the importance of taking medication regularly. They are assessed with regard to whether the family is "high expressed emotion" (bad) or "low expressed emotion" (less bad) and are instructed in techniques to promote family harmony and calm communication. But never in any of these programs is the notion that anyone might have anything to do with poor behaviors beyond the biologically flawed person displaying schizophrenic symptoms. This is an illness, we are reminded over and over again. It is nobody's fault.

Well, maybe. That is, schizophrenia—to be redundant—does in fact have some biological underpinnings. However, cross-cultural studies demonstrate that certain cultural conditions must be in place for schizophrenic symptoms to emerge in any particular individual, regardless of genetic makeup. Most significantly, schizophrenic behavior seems to be enacted in societies that are chaotic, individualistic, and undergoing rapid cultural change either from internal or external influences. In slower-moving, family-oriented societies, there appears to be a lower reported incidence of schizoid behaviors. Worldwide, schizophrenia seems to occur on average in about 0.7% of any given human population (WHO n.d.); yet in the United States, the current diagnosed rate for all forms of schizophrenia listed in DSM IV is about 1.1%, according to the National Institute of Mental Health (2008). Why does the United States have nearly twice as many reported schizophrenics than the average?

It is because we rely on the medical model and the psychotherapeutic metaphor. Instead of insisting that, first, all of us have a part to play in encouraging crazy behavior, and that, second, families, neighborhoods, and communities more specifically have some responsibility, we instead argue that psychotic behavior is the result of an internal flaw in the individual sufferer. We drug the sufferer and do not change the conditions that elicit the behavior to begin with. We blame the psychotic and do nothing to make things better so that psychotic behaviors are less likely to emerge in the future. Modern psychopharmacology and the psychotherapeutic metaphor make such unconscionable reactions comfortable.

It's so depressing

Only very recently has the assertion been made that depression may be a culture bound syndrome as well. It is almost axiomatic in the United States: depression is a disease that requires pharmaceutical treatment to cure. Significant work has been done allegedly outlining the clear biodynamics of depression, and an entire suite of drugs has been added to the physician's toolbox to treat depression. The unfortunate reality is that these anti-depressants just don't work (Laurance 2008).

If that's the case, then the belief that depression is solidly and, perhaps, only biologically based has to be incorrect as well. Again, those whose faith in the biomedical model has been shaken will aver, sometimes with great hostility, that it isn't that anti-depressants don't work—it's just that the science has yet to catch up with the disease, so that the drugs are not yet sophisticated enough. Or, they'll cry, they know plenty of people, including themselves, on whom anti-depressants do work (and woe betide anyone who mentions the placebo effect to these believers). Or, they say, the research declaring anti-depressants to be ineffective is fatally flawed. Nowhere can these American believers in the biological model ever make room for the fact that depression may be culture-bound like so many other behaviors.

It is clear that, depending on how the condition is understood within a culture, the behaviors associated with and called "depression" could be understood as a blessing from the spiritual world, allowing for visions and other supernatural phenomena. So much of what we do is so strongly shaped by culture. The West sees it as an unfortunate affliction. That would tend to shape a sufferer's experience of depression. If it is a desired state, why on earth would you try to cure it? And if it conflicts with the dominant cultural script—as it does in America, land of happiness and dreams—it does make sense that we would try to control depression, or behaviors that look like depression, as much as we can. Because of the medical model under which we operate, pathologizing lethargy, sadness, and other depressive symptoms thus requires a biological explanation and a biological cure.

As is becoming painfully obvious, moreover, the psychopharmaceutical solution is becoming more and more troubling, given the extremely poor track record of most anti-psychotics and neuroleptics (at best effective in perhaps 30% of the cases for schizophrenias). However, the literature with which I am familiar involving

South and Southeast Asia indicates that a short-term course of anti-psychotics in the treatment of an acute psychotic episode for what we would call schizophrenia seems effective—if the sufferer has family and community with him or her all the time for the first month or so. People actually seem to be cured of schizophrenia in such situations—unlike the West, in which the diagnosis determines the life course, as discussed before. Arthur Kleinman (Kleinman and Good 1985) has written quite eloquently about depression, and Richard Castillo (1997) has more generally interesting things to say about brain plasticity and labeling theory as determining the course of the experience of schizophrenia in the West and otherwise. It is not a stretch to argue that the experience of depression, too, is at the very least shaped by culture.

The anthropological literature as well makes quite a distinction between those feeling states as "diagnosed" by Western medicine—which in themselves are understood by many anthropologists as cultural constructions and folk theories at best—that privilege the emotional expression of distress as opposed to other theories of distress that privilege the somatic. So China understands neurathensia, for instance, as something very different than depression. But westerners would call it that—wrongly, in my view, as the theories of emotional experience and etiology of depression and of neurathensia are completely different.

Hikikomori—which is a new phenomenon in Japan, involving young adults shutting themselves off from the world by staying in their rooms for years at a time but being completely supported in this by their parents (who continue to feed and house them)—again could be read by westerners as depression, but it is far more complex than that. Like depression in the West, cultural factors are tremendously important in shaping the experience. Only in a relatively wealthy society, with relatively wealthy families, could this incredibly selfish behavior be tolerated. Since unproductive behavior is being rewarded, we have to assume that the labor of the young men who are hikikomori is less than necessary. The journalist Michael Zielenziger (2006) has written an interesting, if rambling and somewhat ethnocentric, account of this in *Shutting Out the Sun*. Similarly, it could be argued that depression is certainly not a worldwide phenomenon. We see its manifestations in the West but it is not at all clear that we see it among, for instance, the !Kung of Botswana or various groups in New Guinea or other folks in Africa. See Meredith Small's *The Culture of Our Discontent* (2006) for some discussion of this. And explain, if you can, how the Bangladeshi can have been ranked, by surveys reported by the BBC recently, as the happiest people on earth. You would think that they, amongst almost everyone, have the most to be depressed about, but no.

Although anthropologists have been arguing for a number of years now that the experience and enactment of suffering—whether it is depression, schizophrenia, or some other behavior suite—is culturally shaped at the very least, those who share American culture unreflectively seem very threatened by this notion. If, in fact, depression as understood in the folk theories of emotion that Americans share (and, to be honest, that folk theory is not very less sophisticated than that outlined in DSM) is something that we created, if it is something that is culture-bound and learned, then it is a set of behaviors that can be unlearned without pharmaceuticals (which, again, appear not to work all that well). Such a notion is fought bitterly, however, by those who, one would think, do not have much of a stake in it. The reality is, however, that to work to effect a change in culture of this magnitude—to really keep depression from being exhibited as much as it is now—would be a huge effort, and it does not appear to be one that many Americans wish to take on right now. It is much easier to suggest pills and individual psychotherapy, apparently.

The notion that westerners feel the overwhelming need to categorize behavior of other societies as exactly like ours is troubling at best (and Catherine Lutz addressed it in, among other things, her 1985 essay "Depression and the Translation of Emotional Worlds"—so this is not a new idea). Neurasthenia is not depression, as we understand it, though westerners keep insisting on calling it that. It is a set of physical symptoms; the emotional piece is irrelevant, as an element of healing discourse

The impulse to place individual blame on troublesome behaviors, so that only individual "cures" are possible, is a profoundly politically conservative act. Behaviors are socially and culturally created and the best solutions are those that involve a sufferer's social networks. Certainly drugs are not the solution—and, anyway, we're seeing that they seem pretty much ineffective for most troublesome behaviors.

We're all mentally ill

This leads to a disquieting conclusion: if each of us looks long enough and hard enough, we will discover that we display some set of symptoms described in DSM IV. In other words, we're all mentally ill. We can't be grumpy; we suffer from mood dysphoric disorder (and yes, there are drugs to alleviate that). We aren't grieving for loved ones who have died; we have major depression (situational) (yes, drugs can help with that too). Teenagers who don't obey aren't snot-nosed brats; they have contracted defiant oppositional disorder (yup, drugs again). We can't even have a fight with our spouses; under a new category being proposed for DSM V (due out in 2010), the relationship is sick, having gotten Relationship Disorder (Kirn 2002: 92) (drugs, yes, and psychotherapy, fully billable).

This is the psychotherapeutic metaphor distilled to its finest essence. No behavior is normal. Upset emotions are judged to require treatment just as an upset tummy does, or it can lead to the psychological equivalent of esophageal cancer for untreated heartburn (Szasz makes a similar though not identical argument [2007]). Boomers and their children have been taught to carefully monitor their emotional states. If anything is out of whack, get thee to a therapist and get diagnosed. It's not clear, however, that this is good either for individuals or for American society.

Narcissism and the good society

One thing psychotherapists seem concerned about lately is the huge upswing in clients who display symptomology described as either narcissistic personality disorder or borderline personality disorder (Kutchins and Kirk 1997: 176–199). One reason for concern is that these are incredibly obnoxious, difficult clients. They whine, they're overly dependent, they never leave therapy, they never seem to get better, and drugs simply do not work on these people. They believe the world revolves around them and they like to upset that world so that everyone pays attention to them and sees how smart, beautiful, insightful, and generally wonderful they are. In fact, they are incredibly boring to be around; the more they display their symptoms, the more people move away from them. Those displaying borderline and narcissistic personality disorder symptoms then try to move closer, never understanding why nobody likes them. There are many, many people displaying these behaviors in the past twenty years or so. Some mental health professionals believe that borderline personality disorder emerges in abusive families, although there is absolutely no verifiable evidence for this. Narcissistic behavior, on the other hand, seems most common in men. Though no biological factors have yet been identified, don't worry: researchers are working hard on doing so.

What no one seems to be considering is that these are clearly connected to dominant American culture. We have built a culture based on individual self-aggrandizement and a concentration on oneself and one's needs rather than applauding others and paying attention to their wants. We are encouraged to constantly be emotionally self-aware, and to express that regardless of what others might want to be doing. Our fingers are on our own emotional pulse, but we seem unaware of whether anyone else is even breathing, much less taking her emotional pulse for her. We have abandoned our communities, our neighbors, our families in our search for personal fulfillment and self-esteem. It is no wonder that narcissistic and borderline personality disorders are being discussed as much as they are. It is the end result of an infantile culture that insists that each and every individual is important all the time. My needs must always come first. I must never sacrifice for someone else, or even shut up for someone else. It is not individuals who should be "diagnosed" with narcissistic or borderline personality disorders: it is all of us, and our culture of which we are so uncritical.

We are number one

Current dominant American culture and associated political maneuverings are connected to the notion that everyone is a narcissist. From the horrors of September 11, 2001 emerged a Bush administration construction: you may not question us. To inquire about the "War on Terrorism" is unpatriotic, apparently a bad thing. To even raise a question about the Bush administration's effectiveness abroad borders on the treasonous. Everyone in the world wants our values, our way of life, our family constructions, our allegedly democratic system. The world wants to be America; only universals exist; there are no cultural differences of any importance except those imposed on hapless peoples (yearning to breathe free) by despotic dictators or wild-eyed Islamic terrorists. The Bush administration is unapologetic about its horrifically and dangerous ethnocentrism. Might makes right, Dick Cheney all but told us. We have the best government in the world and anyone who says otherwise is a terrorist sympathizer.

If that's not narcissism, I don't know what is. Our government, including the strangely subdued Congress, and our media do not seem to question these precepts all that often. Instead, we seem to go along with the proposition offered: If I think it's true, it must be true. I'm smart and so I know better than anyone else. If you challenge me, there's something wrong with you, not with what I'm saying. This is an infantile, immoral stance. No wonder our culture is in the shape that it is, when government asserts such things and our media do not challenge them.

Narcissists and borderline personality disorder sufferers just hate to be challenged. A challenge becomes for them a personal attack rather than an intellectual difference. And American culture nurtures such responses. If we are all mentally ill, it is in large part due to the larger culture we have created that encourages belly-button gazing, self-involvement, and infantile behavior. We need to stop it. Now.

Chapter 8

Color Blind Hearts and Minds

There is an elephant in the room that is this book. We have danced daintily around an enormous truth that is interwoven with all the various other truths making up the suffering of so many in this country. And that gigantic reality is what is glossed as "race" in this country. The fact of bigotry and discrimination remains a powerful variable in all the social problems discussed in earlier chapters. And, of course, this fact is put, almost exclusively, in psychotherapeutic and hyperindividualistic terms. Bigotry and discrimination, couched as they are so often in terms of flawed or virtuous interiorities, are discussed in this society, by the Left anyway, as though all that is needed is some kind of education (or reeducation). The Right argues, in contrast, that bigotry and discrimination are largely relics of the past, due in large part lately, they say, to the horror of affirmative action. It is now "white" people against whom discrimination is active, and, in particular, "white" men. Once more, nowhere in any of these discussions, except very lightly by the Left and, almost unheard, by members of some ethnicities (Pitts 2008) is there a demand for fundamental, structural change.

Before we can get there, though, the entire concept of "race" needs unpacking. First, we'll look at the reality that "race" is a useless concept in many ways given human history and prehistory. Then we will briefly explore the legacy of racism on both individual and institutional levels in this country. Finally we'll discuss the concepts of bigotry and discrimination as they are understood using the psychotherapeutic metaphor, concluding that behavior needs changing (starting with the replacement of "race" with "ethnicity"). Now, to a potted history of human evolution.

The myth of "race"

The conventional folk definition of "race" in the United States seems to include the following components: that "race" indicates groups separated by significant biological, physiological, and genetic variation; that the genetic variation and thus group membership can be identified through skin color; and that somehow this group membership and genetic commonality translates into distinctive behavioral, cognitive, and emotional patterns, or separate cultures for each group (Brues 1997). More sophisticated thinkers argue that this last component—distinctive "cultures"—are real and salient differences between "racial" groups and should be investigated, explored, appreciated (or, at least, tolerated), and respected. Those same thinkers argue—correctly—that "race" is a series of social, historical, economic, and cultural constructions; but the basic information demonstrating the mythical nature of the first two components is rarely discussed. Here we need to fill in the gaps in our knowledge about the very concept of "race" through discussion of the powerful evolutionary evidence gathered by anthropologists, biologists, biochemists, and other scientists. Race does not exist in any meaningful biological or behavioral way.

First: we are all African. Anthropologists have discovered in the past decade or so that all modern humans—*Homo sapiens sapiens*—come from an original population in southern and eastern Africa. Indeed, all human life and ancestral humans (that is, hominids) originated in Africa (the discussion in this section is derived from, in part, the following works: Diamond 1992; Fagan 2004; Kuper 1996; Marks 2003; Oppenheimer 2004; Scott 2004; Shreeve 1995; and Tattersall 2002). We know this through examination of evidence on several fronts (though it should be noted that not all anthropologists agree with this evidence and the conclusions drawn from it; further, note that dates for fossil evidence are gained through stratigraphy [relative dating] and carbon-14 and other absolute dating methods as well as through blood work and DNA testing).

First, fossil evidence seems clear: physical structures in hominid skeletons indicate various changes over millions of years. Modern humans look somewhat different from our very first hominid ancestors, the *Austrolopithicines*, who first appear on the scene roughly 4.5 million years ago (note: we are not descended from the apes—or monkeys, for that matter—but instead apes [chimpanzees and gorillas] share a common ancestor with humans). Briefly, as any introductory anthropology text can tell you (such as Chapter 4 of Kottak 2008; Roberts 2005; or Feder 2003), *Austrolopithecines* were shorter than us, had smaller brains and a slightly different skeletal shape—but they walked upright and had the attendant pelvic, back, neck, and foot structure to prove it. We find *Austrolopithecines* only in Africa, though they persisted for a very long period of time, a good 3 million years. Next comes *Homo habilis*, who appears in Africa about 2 million years ago and seems to have been around a relatively short 400,000 years and overlapping with the last of the *Austrolopithecines, A. bosei*. Following *habilis* is *Homo erectus*, appearing in African roughly 1.6 million years ago and sticking around for nearly 1.5 million years, coexisting (though probably not in the same habitat) with *Homo habilis*. The evidence suggests that some *Homo erectus* stayed in Africa, while others migrated as far as the eastern coast of Asia. Ultimately, however, *Homo erectus* was extinguished as a species perhaps around 300,000 years ago, when *Homo sapiens* (archaic) and *Homo sapiens neanderthalenis* began to take over. Evidence of archaic *Homo sapiens* appears in Africa, Asia, and Europe; fossils span a relatively small time period of 300,000 to 35,000 years ago. In that span, *Homo sapiens neanderthalenis* evolves from archaic *Homo sapiens*, though we only see Neanderthal in Europe and parts of the Middle East—it does not appear in Africa or Asia. Finally, *Homo sapiens sapiens*—us, fully modern humans—arrives on the world scene about 100,000 years ago.

The best evidence available suggests that *Homo sapiens sapiens* evolved from *Homo erectus* in southern and eastern Africa beginning approximately 110,000 years ago and quickly migrated throughout the contiguous land masses that we now call Europe, African, and Asia. *Homo sapiens sapiens* appeared in Australia from southeast Asia and Indonesia approximately 60,000 years ago; *Homo sapiens sapiens* migrated to the Western hemisphere probably somewhere between 60,000 and 15,000 years ago. This means that the indigenous people of Australia and the Americas migrated to those places as fully modern humans.

Neanderthal, by the way, died out while *Homo sapiens sapiens* were migrating through the world. It's unclear exactly why they died out; hypotheses include a lack of adaptive fit between Neanderthal physical and intellectual structures and then-current environmental conditions (the end of the last great Ice Age, which was 75,000–12,000 years ago); the evolutionary superiority of *Homo sapiens sapiens* (which included, among other things, a more efficient brain and speech leading to many other kinds of highly environmentally adaptive behaviors including amazingly accurate group hunting, and shared child care); or, far less plausibly, a more violent set of behaviors by *Homo sapiens sapiens* leading to the wholesale slaughter of Neanderthal.

What all of this tells us is that we are all Africans. All modern humans began in Africa. And there is further evidence to demonstrate this. A number of scholars, most notably James Wainscoat at Oxford and Rebecca Cann, Mark Stoneking, and Allan Wilson at the University of California-Berkeley, have matched DNA from *Homo sapiens sapiens* fossils in Africa to modern humans worldwide today.

More specifically, Cann et al. (1987) examined mitochondrial DNA from many folks around the world. Mitochondria exist either as free-floating entities or within cells. All animal and human cells have mitochondria. It is possible to find the DNA attached to mitochondria; that DNA directs many of the proteins used in cells. When Cann et al. found was that mitochondrial DNA (mtDNA) exists in a woman's eggs but that it disperses from a man's sperm; this means that all animal mtDNA is inherited from the mother and not the father. By looking at the genes present either in ancient DNA or in the blood of modern humans, one can compare genetic structures over time. If the genetic structures of one group of people varies from other groups of people, certain conclusions can be made. For instance, mtDNA mutates much more slowly than nucleic DNA, meaning that the rate of mutation, and the form that those mutations take, is much more easily seen, and because the rate of change is regular, we can approximately our relationship to common ancestors (Shreeve 1995: 63). Furthermore, the majority of those genetic mutations are neutral when it comes to natural selection—they don't affect how the mtDNA works. When we take this slow rate of evolutionary change, along with the fact that mtDNA is provided only by one's mother, and we can note differences among groups with regard to mtDNA, we can chart some very interesting family trees. What Cann et al. have discovered is that mtDNA evidence demonstrates that those family trees all are rooted in Africa. Current humans in Africa seem to have mtDNA rather different than those whose ancestors migrated. In addition, comparison of modern human mtDNA and Neanderthal mtDNA shows that the Neanderthal sequence, while closer to modern humans than to chimps, was outside the range of variation of modern human mtDNA. Neanderthal were *homo sapiens*, to be sure, but not modern humans. This further suggests that modern humans migrated out of Africa; they did not evolve independently in different places.

If, then, modern humans did not evolve independently in different places—Africa, Asia, Europe—then racial groupings (Asians, Africans, Europeans) based on presumed shared genetic heritage do not make any kind of scientific sense. Three simply is no evidence that categories so broad have any utility in understanding human variation.

Indeed, to choose just one outward manifestation of what is presumed to be a shared genetic trait—skin color, the typical American market used to identify "racial" categories—is far too simplistic. There are many outward manifestations, called phenotypes, of genetic makeup. Yet in the United States it is the only one that matters. Such a dichotomous grouping—you are either black or white—is built on cultural dynamics responding to social, political, economic, religious, and historical needs, not on human biology. Why do we not choose other ones? Why do we not choose hair texture? Or eye color? Or lip shape? Or eye shape? Or height, or weight, or the thousands of other phenotypical expressions? It is obvious that the distribution of other kinds of genetic markers—the relative distribution of blood types, for instance, or of sickle-cell anemia—is largely ignored as we continue in our attempts to categorize people into "races."

Anthropologists argue that a far more useful and accurate grouping is that of "cline" or population. A biological population, or cline, is a series of gradations of a genetic trait over a specific geographic range. For instance, we know that the number of people with blood type A lessens the further west you go in Europe—and that someone with blood type B is less likely to contract smallpox than is someone with blood type A (Lieberman and Kirk 1997: 194). The distribution of blood type, something that doesn't have much to do with evolutionary environmental pressures, is clearly an expression of a genetic trait, and a discussion of clines is far more useful than that of race in this instance.

This is also true for sickle cell anemia. We know that sickle cell anemia is an adaptation to malaria—the sickling pattern of blood cells seems to help protect the human body from the parasite causing malaria. We would expect, then, that sickle cell anemia could be a widespread condition in potentially or actually malarial environments. What we see is a distribution that puts sickle cell anemia most frequently in populations in West Africa; but, intriguingly, it appears as well in Mediterranean populations, in South Asian populations, and in Southeast Asia (indeed, it is not a mistake that the gin and tonic was probably created by the British while occupying India—the quinine in tonic water protects against malaria [Kasper 2007]). Sickle cell anemia, then, is not a "black" disease as it often has been called. Instead, it crosses what have been naively thought to be "racial" lines, afflicting Africans and African Americans, to be sure, but Italians, Armenians, Turks, Arabs, Slavs living along the Adriatic Sea, Indians and Sri Lankans, Laotians, Vietnamese, Indonesians, as well. "Race" does not explain genetic variation.

Even if we try to use skin color to group people, we quickly find it a useless exercise. The range in variation of skin tone—which, as we know, in humans is a small difference in shades of brown—appears to be more distinctive within what have been thought of as "racial" groups. The skin tone of North Africans is quite different than that of Africans in the south, or in Central Africa. And the traditionally nomadic !Kung, called, insultingly, Bushman or the San (a Xhosa word for enemy), have a skin tinged with yellowish brown. Yet they are Africans. They are not black. South Asians—Indians, particularly in the south of India, and Sri Lankans—tend to have dark brown skin. They are not currently Africans, yet they are "black." Australian aborigines as well have dark brown skin. They are not currently Africans, yet they are "black." So skin color doesn't help us understand the human experience; it is merely a biological adaptation to environments with lots of sunlight. It doesn't tell us anything about who these folks are. If we decided to use a different phenotype—hair texture, or nose shape, or lip fullness, or eye shape—we would find much greater variation within the group, crossing skin color lines. Our folk categories of race are inaccurate in that they assume homogeneity (that is, complete genetic identicalness) and hide the profound variations that exist within these simplistic groupings. There is no gene for "race," anyway. Phenotypical expressions of genes—hair, eye color, pigmentation, lip shape, and so forth—vary independently, not as a cluster of genes.

So why do we hang on to these groupings? Earlier, I said that our folk theory of "race" signifies groups separated by significant biological, physiological, and genetic variation, and that the genetic variation and thus groups membership can be identified through skin color, and that somehow this group membership and genetic commonality translates into distinctive behavioral, cognitive, and emotional patterns. More sophisticated thinkers, I went on to say, say that this last component—distinctive "cultures"—are real and salient differences between "racial" groups that should be investigated, explored, appreciated (or, at least, tolerated), and respected. These same thinkers argue—correctly—that "race" is a series of social, historical, economic, and cultural constructions.

How do such things get constructed? In part, in its pseudobiological form, anyway, it has to do with European exploration (Liberman and Kirk 1997) and classification of people on the basis on skin color (Brues 1997: 191–192). Upon encountering those who appear to be different—because they look different in one way—Europeans decided that Europeans were superior and that the "natives" were inferior. A complex hierarchy of these peoples began to be constructed by Europeans so that by the mid-1800s it was possible for Europeans (and more specifically the British) to say with a straight face that three categories of people existed: the savages, the barbarians, and the civilized. Typically, savages were Africans, native Australians, and American Indians (who, due to European technological superiority [e.g., guns, germs, and ocean-going boats; see Diamond 1999], were massacred and/or enslaved in huge numbers), barbarians were most Asians (who could not be conquered by Europeans given that their level of technology and hubris nearly matched that of Europeans), and, of course, the civilized were the Europeans, with the British at the pinnacle. The understanding of race we currently hold is derived directly from colonialist oppression and exploitation.

It is time we abandoned the concept. It is time we begin to understand the complexity of human variation, and it is time to embark on a new nomenclature, that of ethnicity, when trying to understand human behavioral, emotional, and cognitive variation. Race, with its pseudoscientific, biologistic baggage, clouds rather than illuminates the human experience.

The rest of "them"

It surely cannot be denied that the United States is a strongly racist society; we also are well aware of ethnic differences between us. This is particularly true in Northern cities, so that one's ethnic affiliation as well as one's "racial" appearance is assumed to shape one's identity on a biological level. Being able to identify someone as Polish American or Italian American seems, for many people (especially in my hometown of Chicago), to be an important thing. We assume that certain behavioral characteristics or worldviews accompany that identity, just as the dominant European American culture makes assumptions about what all African Americans believe, or what all Latinos do. Holding stereotypical beliefs about ethnic and "racial" groups is, on the one hand, a rather human characteristic—there are few societies that do not draw differentiations between groups of people. However, this usually occurs in a more unitary, identifiably homogeneous group. The U.S. European American majority is by no means homogeneous; certainly European Americans do not agree with each other on many major issues. What this means is that differentiation, identifying people by "racial" or ethnic markers, is a fundamentally human practice. The consequences of that practice can vary widely, though. In the United States, as in South Africa, Rwanda-Burundi, Brazil, Germany, France, Vietnam, Northern Ireland, and many other countries that have a large, powerful, dominant class (the majority, in sociological lingo) and various powerless ethnic or "racial" minorities, the dominant class resists change that would provide equal access to opportunity and power. That is, those in power generally and understandably want to remain in power; the status quo is desirable; and policies that, although perhaps not specifically racist but which effectively bar people from climbing the economic ladder, are maintained.

In order to do this, significant differences between people must be asserted, justifying separate treatment. That is, in the United States, the dominant European American majority has believed (and many continue to believe) that African Americans, Latinos, Asian Americans, and American Indians (as well as significant numbers of South Asians, Arabs, and Eastern Europeans) are fundamentally different than "the rest of us." One way to valorize that is to declare certain groups as separate "races" even though, as shown above, the concept is biologically false. Nonetheless, the concept of "race" remains very powerful, and not just in the United States. In Northern Ireland, for instance, Protestants and Catholics will argue occasionally that they are separate races and that's why they don't get along. These are northern Europeans with little outside genetic material coming in—that is, the biological reality shows that statement to be ridiculous. They're all Irish, or, at most, Celtic, part of a complex of a northern European biological population that shares some physical characteristics. Yet they insist on creating significant differences among what are objectively speaking quite similar groups. "Race," then, is culturally defined, not biologically salient. In the United States, those differences form the basis for exaggerating what are quite minor differences between the majority and everyone else—and of course this process leads to serious maltreatment of all kinds of people.

When European Americans promote "racial" differences, they are, in essence, failing to recognize their own immense "white privilege," as scholars sometimes call it. It's not necessary, if you are European American, to think about your ethnic identity, unless you choose to so identify yourself. In European American day-to-day cultural preferences—food, music, clothing, sports, hairstyles—the great majority of European Americans display no particular ethnic identity. Those in minority groups, however, are constantly called on to think about their ethnic identities as they make decisions about where to live, how to walk, what to study, where to shop. Indeed, as Peggy McIntosh points out in her article "White Privilege: Unpacking the Invisible Knapsack" (1988), European Americans are blind to institutional bigotry on small, personal ways.

McIntosh points out fifty different ways that European Americans experience privilege; some are significant and some are so mundane as to be laughable. For instance, McIntosh points out that European Americans are rarely, if ever, asked for the European American point of view of a subject, unlike African Americans, who are constantly required to represent their entire ethnic group. European Americans, she notes, can buy "flesh colored" bandaids that will actually match their flesh. European Americans can be quite sure that, if they go into a supermarket, they will find hair-care products appropriate for their hair. And they can look at apartments and houses with great surety that, if they like the place, they will not be rejected on the basis of their ethnicity. And the list goes on.

McIntosh's list, though twenty years old, remains material to American culture today. European Americans are underrepresented on the welfare rolls. They are arrested, incarcerated, and executed at lower rates than African Americans and Latinos. European Americans have access, by and large, to better schools, better housing, better supermarkets, better neighborhoods, better credit availability, better transportation, and better just about everything else than the minorities in our culture. European Americans start the race of life far ahead of minorities (again, for the most part; there certainly are some European American populations with significant barriers in their way, particularly in poverty-stricken Appalachia, but even those populations begin ahead of poverty-stricken African American and Latino groups).

Minority groups in the United States, on the other hand, remain relatively powerless, largely through systemic discrimination and through the idea that each such group is a unitary whole, despite wide diversity within each group. There are, of course, some similar experiences for minority groups, especially for African Americans who face overt institutionalized discrimination every single day. Pitts (2008) points out, for instance, the absolute likelihood—indeed, the reality—that young African American men will be pulled over by the police for offences that would be ignored if the young man was European American. Ask any African American man about DWB ("driving while black") and he will verify that he has committed this offence. DWB is a process resulting from institutionalized discrimination that reminds African Americans constantly of their ethnic identity, again in ways that European Americans do not have to worry about. This marginalization, this disempowerment of minorities in the United States is a long-standing practice. Why? There are a number of theories to explain the experience of discrimination and bigotry—deficiency theories, prejudice and bigotry, and institutional racism.

Deficiency theories include arguments that are spurious at best. For instance, there are "scholars" out there who assert that minority groups are, by and large, simply dumber that European Americans. While certainly this was the position held by mightily ignorant Europeans during the colonialist period, it is astounding that this set of ideas gets any traction. However, Charles Murray and the late Michael Herrnstein certainly asserted such things to great acclaim (Herrnstein and Murray 1994). Herrnstein built a career on arguing, in appallingly social Darwinist ways, that smarter people are richer and that poor people, because they are stupid, are poor. This cannot be changed and, in fact, according to this hypothesis, this is congruent with nature. There is no point in trying to better the lot of the poor. The Bell Curve (ibid.) argues, in essence, that African Americans are genetically inferior as proven by IQ tests and therefore any attempt to help African Americans out of poverty—such as affirmative action or education involving liberal arts subjects or advanced training—is a waste of time, money, and effort.

Now, the reality is that African Americans do, on average, score fifteen points lower on many IQ tests than do European Americans. Herrnstein and Murray's conclusions about this, however, have been challenged on a number of grounds (Fischer et al. 1996). Claude Fischer and his colleagues argue that Herrnstein and Murray's work is fatally flawed. For instance, they point out—correctly—that IQ tests are not a very good test of intelligence; most psychometricians would agree. In terms of real and applicable intelligence, there are few good testable parameters. While certainly some people are, in fact, smarter than other people, conventional IQ tests can't measure those differences too well. What they can test and predict is a person's future success in school. Social class, then, and access to reasonable schools from preschool on up resulting from one's class position, would interact with IQ. Interestingly, Fischer and his colleagues, using Herrnstein and Murray's own data, found a strong correlation between social class and IQ score; ethnic background or a presumed genetic commonality seemed to have little to do with it.

Socioeconomic status seems to predict future poverty, not IQ (and not ethnic identity). Your current class position is a very reliable indicator of class position in the future. It is social stratification, and not intelligence of individuals, that most strongly determines your future economic well being. Rather than assigning fault for poverty to individuals because they are just not smart enough, Fischer et al. pretty clearly show that poverty is the result of widespread systemic inequality. This seems to be played out by evidence from other societies.

Irish immigrants in England, Koreans in Japan, different groups of Jews in Israel, Afrikaaners in South Africa...all groups score lower on standardized tests of IQ (Fischer et al. 1996: 192–193) yet all seem to be members of biological population very similar to the majority. How can it be, if IQ, tied to ethnicity and biology, predicts future success and well being? Well, Fischer et al. (and many other analysts) argue that it can't. In other words, the notion that minorities in the United States (and elsewhere) suffer from discrimination and differential lack of resources is not because the minorities are deficient. It is because the society is deficient—racist, bigoted, discriminatory.

In addition, Herrnstein and Murray and those who promote their analysis seem to believe that there are a number of genetically isolated breeding pools in the United States, and that those groups are identifiable as "black," "white," and so forth. This is a mightily impoverished discussion given the history of slavery in this country. African Americans in particular clearly were subjected to rape or other kinds of involuntary sexual activity by European Americans throughout the shame of slavery. There is no more a biologically isolated "race" of African Americans than there is of European Americans. To argue, as The Bell Curve authors do, that "blacks" constitute some sort of separate population with defective genetics is, quite simply, wrong. If the analysis is to be rejected—and it is, in its entirety—the basic assumption made here of some kind of separate breeding group invalidates the entire discussion on its face.

One issue that such a discussion elicits, though, is whether there is a "black" culture that is distinct from the dominant culture that harms African Americans. While certainly experiences of bigotry are shared among African Americans (and Latinos and, in some places, Asian Americans), thus creating something of a culture, it is very hard to argue that African American culture constitutes a wholly separate experience. Certainly attempts have been made to explain differential access to resource based on an indictment of African American "culture." Those attempts are also flawed.

For instance, more than forty years ago, the late Daniel Patrick Moynihan issued his by now famous "Moynihan Report" in 1965 (Moynihan 1965). A conservative sociologist, Moynihan, at the request of President Lyndon Johnson, examined the state of ethnic relations in an attempt to help promote equality and change. Moynihan argued that African Americans were in the unequal position that they were in during the 1960s because of what he thought of as a defective culture that discouraged working and encouraged out of wedlock births and discouraged marriage. However, Moynihan started out by saying that these behavior phenomena were the direct result of long-standing, intense socioeconomic discrimination against African Americans. However misrepresented Moynihan's work was and still is (and that this has happened is indisputable), it did spark a fair amount of research about the nature of ethnic groups. Much of that research showed that members of such groups, are, in fact, motivated to work and so forth. There has been little research looking at systemic and structural factors which contribute to or cause minority group subordination, however; the focus of research has remained the specific groups in question, so that deficiency theories remain the norm for trying to understand the position of minority groups today.

Another set of theories discussing the position of minority groups in America today has to do with prejudice and bigotry. Some folks say that European Americans are overwhelmingly racist and consumed by bigotry, and that prejudice has caused the poor position of minority groups. Specifically, working-class European Americans harbor deep hatred toward minorities and that hatred keeps minority groups down. There are problems with such assertions, of course. One is that working-class European Americans have only slightly more power in our economic system than the people they hate. Indeed, it could be argued that it is that very real inferior position that causes working-class European Americans to be so bigoted. Working-class European Americans are losing ground, losing jobs, and losing their homes; it is convenient to blame this on minorities who, in their eyes, receive special preferential treatment in hiring, housing, and welfare, instead of blaming corporate capitalism for their unemployment, they blame a much easier and much more identifiable target: African Americans, Latinos, and women (see the documentary *Blood in the Face* [Bohlen et al. 1991] for some interesting insights).

European American prejudice doesn't explain, however, why unprejudiced European Americans (presumably there are some) defend the economic and social arrangements that support institutional racism. An individual European American person may not be overtly bigoted, but she may support tax cuts, subsidies for corporations, pork barrel projects for the home districts of representatives that reward European American voters—things that contribute to the continuing poor socioeconomic conditions of minorities. Why? By supporting the status quo, by not reorganizing the socioeconomic system so that everyone has a truly equal shot, the privileged position of that person is reinforced. While it's perfectly understandable that person wants to maintain her own standard of living, the effect is discriminatory and racist.

So we come back to institutional racism as the reason for the poor position of minority groups in the United States. It almost doesn't matter what people actually believe about minorities or majorities; our socioeconomic system is set up so that, without a big change, racism is the inevitable result of our current practices. That is, the allocation of resources—through federal, state, and local tax dollars—is fundamentally unfair and inequitable. Inner city schools are inadequately supported, but politicians tout tax cuts. Inner city hospitals are closing, but politicians want to cut funding further and promote the private sector in health care (thankfully, though, the pendulum is swinging to the left on issues of health care). Welfare has been decimated, job training programs are being eliminated, housing subsidies have been drastically reduced; all of these were designed to level the playing field, but institutional racism is ensuring that the European American rich will get richer and the poor minorities will remain poor. Although the rhetoric and reasoning behind this "economic plan" sounds rational and objective, in fact the system is clearly racist and prejudiced, so that corporations receive gigantic grants and tax breaks from federal and state coffers while individual welfare is cut. As a whole, corporations get hundreds of billions of dollars (not counting the corporations being paid for their efforts in Iraq) while TANF costs the United States $16.5 billion (Child Welfare League of America n.d.). Welfare comprises a small fraction of the federal budget but it continues to be cut, and cut, and cut, while the administration's friends are rewarded with monthly stipends of millions of dollars; indeed, Kellogg, Brown and Root (KBR), one of the primary private contractors in Iraq, had billables equaling the entire TANF budget (AFP 2007). These facts alone demonstrate the fundamental unfairness and institutionalized racism of America's public policy.

Other things do as well. Our society is generally set up to favor European Americans. This is true historically, in that our country was founded with racist policies already in place. This meant that African Americans and American Indians, from the outset, were excluded from the table (as were all women) on "scientific," political, philosophical, and religious grounds, the remains of which are still with us today. Our belief in the primacy of private property and individual rights means that although political citizenship can be had (now that, theoretically, everyone can own property), we have a very poor understanding of social citizenship. We understand our rights, but we have a very underdeveloped understanding of our responsibilities to our fellow citizens (and especially noncitizens). This stems from our history, of course.

Our current system is based on European American middle class norms. Though those norms are not necessarily bad, they are not neutral and certainly minority group members have difficulty accessing the means to attain those norms. It is institutional racism that prevents minorities from meeting reasonable expectations from schools and employers.

It is sometimes hard to see institutional discrimination and racism. One must really look at the ramifications of our current socioeconomic system in order to see the results. Individual racism—burning crosses, DWB, concentrating drug arrests on small-time dealers instead of the major distributors, or European Americans for that matter, using racial epithets—is obvious and, for most of us, socially unacceptable behavior, whether it comes from individuals in the majority or in the minority (Louis Farrakhan, for instance, is distrusted by European Americans because of his overt racism and hostility).

Institutional racism is so difficult, finally, because it involves a number of different social institutions. Poor education leads to poor job prospects; an employer does not want to employ poorly educated people and so leaves his inner city location, leading to further unemployment and the further deterioration of inner city schools, neighborhoods, and job bases. Minority stereotypes are reinforced by employer experience and by media portrayals.

Bigotry by any other name

It's important, as we think about these issues, to parse out the meanings of various terms. Bigotry is one of these terms that has broad applicability in a myriad of situations. Quite simply, bigotry is an emotional, social, or intellectual stance held by an individual. That stance is a profoundly stereotypical, prejudiced attitude about groups of people based on assumptions rather than facts. Bigotry allows for no nuance, for no sophistication and is learned from others. Now, it could be fairly said that some form of stereotyping is part of the human condition: we have to be able to predict the behaviors of others, and we do that based on partial scripts of what we've learned to expect from various types of people. Bigotry, though, never lets any further information in. The categories are fixed and evidence that may contradict the bigot's view is ignored. Finally, bigotry often (though not always) leads to discrimination, at least when the bigot is part of the majority. Bigotry, then, is profoundly individual (though based on cultural understandings) and is most often the subject of study when trying to understand racism (see, e.g., Wormer 1997: 14–17).

Discrimination

Discrimination, on the other hand, is, quite simply, treating members of a group differently than members of another group for no reason other than group membership. This may mean that an African American is watched with suspicion in department stores while European Americans can shop without fear (McIntosh 1988), for instance. It means that members of one group get preferential treatment while members of other groups are barred from housing, employment, school systems, and the like. Bigotry is about attitudes; discrimination is about actions.

As any introductory sociology course will tell you, Robert Merton very famously outlined four types of bigotry and discrimination. He argued that social norms will shape how individuals think and act about majorities and minorities. Merton discussed the prejudiced discriminator, a bigot who acts on his stereotypes whenever possible. There is the unprejudiced nondiscriminator, someone who holds no stereotypes and does not discriminate regardless of societal conditions. But then there is the prejudiced nondiscriminator, something of a puzzle, and, even more puzzling, the unprejudiced discriminator. How can those last two types make sense?

Merton said that, in fact, this makes a great deal of sense depending on social conditions. If someone who is prejudiced nonetheless recognizes that acting on those prejudices through discriminatory behavior will garner trouble, that person will not discriminate no matter how much she wants to. Similarly, someone who has no bigotry may find that, for economic or social survival, he must discriminate ("everyone else is doing it"). Therefore, it's clear that paying attention solely to attitudes when trying to fight prejudice and discrimination is a recipe for failure. Attitudes don't seem to harm people. Discrimination does, actively.

Yet most attempts to fight racism deal almost exclusively with "hearts and minds." In particular, liberals argue that education is the key to fighting prejudice. (Conservatives don't seem to care much about this issue.) Apparently if all of those mean old bigots just understood the facts, they would be tolerant and not prejudiced any longer. Furthermore, this education is to start in early childhood. Education, though, is the key. The point of this process, then, is to change minds, to help our society become color blind.

Color blind hearts and minds

The liberal attempt, then, ultimately fails over and over again. Discrimination continues, and the overall power structure of the country remains firmly in the hands of the majority. By refusing to engage in a serious discussion of the cultural understandings that lead to active and harmful discrimination, the United States continues to harm minorities in this country. We keep the discussion on the individual, psychological level where, we think, it belongs. Those who are racist need therapy, clearly (see Reich 2000 for an interesting discussion with Peter Kramer on this subject; Kramer affirms that, indeed, racism is a psychological problem). While it would be accurate to say that being the subject of racism is psychologically wounding, the solution for victims of racism is not psychotherapy.

The solution is justice.

Chapter 9

Conclusion

What then do we do? If I am correct, if American culture is dominated by the language of psychotherapy and a commitment to hyperindividualism, what solutions are possible? This language pervades so many parts of our culture. It permeates religion. It is part and parcel of our medical system. It is the foundation, currently, of our educational system. It structures our treatment of adolescents. It controls our understanding of poor behaviors (e.g., "mental illness" and "racism"). It undergirds family life. We see it explored, explained, and enhanced on television and throughout the Internet. It is the lingua franca, by and large, of politics. The language of psychotherapy and hyperindividualism are truly linchpins in American culture. Despite the very serious problems that allegiance to the metaphor and to hyperindividualism poses, we continue to insist, doggedly, that these concepts are the only appropriate ones to understand human behavior. The language of psychotherapy and hyperindividualism clearly shapes the structure of American social policy in ways so that the many social problems Americans face will never be solved. At least, they will not be solved by the continuing use of these concepts. Let's go through the issues one by one.

Child-rearing

One of the first steps needed to continue the discussion of child-rearing is an acknowledgment by all involved that American child-rearing concepts are based pretty much entirely on culture. There is nothing scientific about the practices espoused. Indeed, the suggestions that child development "experts" provide are based fully and thoroughly on folk theories of behavior, motivation, and emotion. Once we admit the contingent nature of our ideas about children and how to rear them, change becomes possible.

One of the most exciting and liberating things about approaching ideas from the standpoint of a cultural anthropologist is the appreciation of the fact that so much of what we do is a human creation. While certainly we are animals ultimately, so much of human behavior is culturally shaped that the biological bases of human existence, while not irrelevant, fade in importance given the power of culture. American culture, then, has created American child-rearing practices for a variety of reasons outlined in this book. Those who share American culture, then, can change those practices.

We can lose the idea, for one thing, that children go through immutable stages of development that involve a growing sense of independence and autonomy. The "terrible twos" and the "fearsome fours" are neither natural nor normal in the context of human behavior worldwide. Instead, these are largely western, and more specifically, American ideas about children. By assigning scientific-sounding titles to what amounts to childish behavior, parents are given an excuse not to discipline their little precious snowflakes. Family psychologist John Rosemond, for one, argues that the abdication of authority by parents has created a generation of little tyrants filled with self-esteem but little actual talent (see www.rosemond.com for some of Dr. Rosemond's views on twenty-first-century child-rearing).

Now, parents across the political and intellectual spectrum will protest. Sure, children ought to be well behaved. But in order for that to happen parents can't just demand that their children act right. A parent has to help the child understand why she must behave well; parents must make sure that children are motivated in the right ways. Furthermore, they would continue, it's mighty old-fashioned to tell children what to do. It's better, they'd say, to explain.

I don't see particularly well-behaved children lately. Explanations are for the benefit of the parent, not the child. Parents seem to want to be friends with their children, following the highly popular television series *Gilmore Girls* (where mom Lorelei considered her daughter Rory to be her best friend, as abcfamily's Web site tells us [2008]). Parents do not want to seem to be adults, as was established in chapter 2. Parents want to play, and everything in the media, as well as many cues from our culture, encourage this profound childishness in adults.

So what's the solution here? Parents, you need to understand that your child-rearing methods are neither "natural" nor "proven." Understand that, in fact, you are harming your child. Even more so, understand that your child-rearing techniques seem to be producing a highly narcissistic, self-involved, deeply selfish, dishonest, and shallow generation. The children being raised today are unlikely to care much about any generation beyond them; the mess that the Bush administration is making of the American economy will not be cleaned up by the children being reared today unless there are significant changes made to how adults view the world. Psychotherapy and hyperindividualism are not answers; they are the problem.

Poverty

Much discussion, hand-wringing, and fury goes into discussions about poverty in this country. What doesn't happen is real work toward a solution. Poverty has been eliminated in many European countries with a simple tool: an equitable tax code and a fair distribution of what is largely unearned wealth. While certainly pockets of poverty exist in wealthy nations for a variety of reasons, Europe has had the courage to do what the United States will not: it taxes the rich, who are rich almost solely because these folks were lucky enough to be born to rich parents (who themselves have their place due to a surfeit of luck). As is true for many in the United States, rich people in Europe did not earn their wealth. They inherited it from people who inherited it. Many of the European rich, however, recognize some things that the American rich do not but should (and, for purposes of this discussion, I define "rich" as anyone earning income or owning assets in the upper 5% of the United States population, or, in 2006, over $170,000 annually [U.S. Census Bureau 2008]). I'll exclude George Soros, Bill Gates, and Warren Buffet from these indictments, however (and Soros is both European and American, which may explain a few things).

What seems to be missing from most of the discussion of poverty in the United States is an acknowledgment—any kind of acknowledgement—that our economic system is a profoundly unjust one, one that causes suffering for reasons that remain spectacularly unclear. Many of those earning exceedingly high incomes (whether from wages or from dividends and interest) come from backgrounds of privilege; not all do, certainly, but Bill Gates (for instance) grew up in a middle-class household. What Gates recognizes that other very wealthy individuals do not, however, is that wealth is earned almost solely due to other people's labor, but it is not often that this labor is paid a living or, better, equitable wage. In other words, the wealthy in America are wealthy directly because of exploitation. And the wealthy often refuse to acknowledge this, moaning instead about taxes and obligations.

Apparently the rich in America believe that the money in their bank accounts is actually theirs, that they earned it somehow, and that it is theirs to do with as they please. The notion that they owe their fellow citizens anything is anathema to the wealthy, by and large, and the idea that they might fulfill their obligations to luck by paying taxes—a higher percentage of taxes on their incomes, not just a higher proportion of the overall tax revenues—appears to be nauseating to many rich people. For example, someone earning \$70,000 might pay approximately 17% of that toward federal income taxes; someone earning \$140,000 pays roughly 25%. A person earning twice as much as someone else only pays 8% more in taxes. It's likely, though, that the wealthier person will complain about his incredibly heavy tax burden. So what we get, instead of justice for all citizens, are tax cuts for the wealthy and effective tax increases on the poor and the middle class. When this is pointed out by the more perspicacious among us, the rich then yelp about "class warfare"—as though they have not been engaged in major battles against the rest of us since the inception of this country.

Instead of accepting at least some part of the structural explanations for poverty in this country, the rich and their handmaidens (academic liberals, social workers, and a number of policy wonks, among others) keep coming up with more and more fantastic explanations for poverty, all of which involving the moral paucity or other deficits of the poor and none of which involving the moral paucity of the wealthy or the deficits of the middle class. No, instead we get "culture of poverty" and "lack of impulse control"—the latter appellation, I pointed out in chapter 3, could be applied to the middle and upper middle classes as well in the United States. This is an amazingly unjust and immoral response to poverty in a country with as much wealth as we have. The solution to poverty is simple: provide a minimum income, high enough to support safe, warm (and cool) housing including utilities, an adequate and healthful diet and clothing, good schooling, adequate transportation, and health care for all in this country. We have no safety net in this society any longer, and it is shameful. In particular, the wealthy should be ashamed of themselves, for their Prada bags and their obsessions with conspicuous consumption. They act in profoundly immoral ways, and they act in disingenuous ways as well, prattling on about their tax burdens when they do not share that burden as equally as they should.

Adolescents

Sharing burdens is something that may help the United States reconfigure our treatment of adolescents. As I pointed out in chapter 4, Americans have created a class of individuals—teenagers—without parallel in human history. The notion that young people should have, by rights, an apprenticeship to adulthood with nearly full adult rights without concomitant responsibilities is astounding. In addition to asserting that young people get to do just about everything adults do, including expressing opinions based on little more than the ability to speak, the United States has decided that children—at least, European American, middle-class children—never misbehave. Instead, they have Oppositional Defiant Disorder, or they are physiologically incapable of getting up shortly after dawn because their brains are just different, or they are Indigo Children expressing their uniqueness. Never in any discussion of troublesome adolescent behavior is a hint that parents may have done a terrible job rearing responsible, respectful children. Never is there a notion that children and young people are not, by and large, mentally ill. Never do we demand that European American young people start acting properly.

No, we assign them mental illnesses—there seems to be a new one every day discussed, with no scientific backing (not that there is any science to psychological diagnosis anyway), in various media ranging from *People Magazine* to the *New York Times*. Poor behavior gets repackaged in the United States as resulting from poor neurology, not morally vacuous parenting. It's too bad that all of this is based solely on some very flimsy folk theories of human behavior and emotion. Parents then aim to befriend rather than parent children, based on popular media portrayals of therapy, psychological diagnoses, and pseudoscientific pronouncements about adolescent blood chemistry and brain structure.

What all of these folks fail to recognize is the fact that, in most parts of the world, young people are up with the sun, contributing economically to the family's well being, taking schoolwork seriously, and finding a way to fit into the family (instead of forcing the family to accommodate them). Adolescence is a created identity, not a "natural" one, despite what psychiatrists and psychologists might say. This is not a stage of development of any significance for the vast majority of human and prehuman history. But by giving adolescents a pass in terms of reasonable behavior, our culture has forgiven parents for their abdication of responsibilities. By psychologizing all teenage action as youthful exuberance that reflects a different physical or neurological reality, by promoting hyperindividualism as expressed through self-esteem promotion, America has created a generation of young people with limited skills, an inability to connect actions and consequences, and a basic dishonesty as seen through plagiarism and self-promotion. While certainly it's accurate to say that many elder generations throughout history have decried The Youth Of Today, American culture's deepening discussion of behavior as genetically, biologically, and, at best, individually based means that the desperate need of members of our society to be able to see connections with one another and with others across the globe is minimal at best. If all we can do is understand ourselves (and then spend many hours explaining that self to everyone else, perhaps on MySpace), the urgent demand to create bonds with many other people will be not met.

In order to reverse some of these very serious deficits among young people today, a set of standards must be upheld in schools, in homes, in churches, and in other venues across the nation. Plagiarism, for instance, must never be tolerated, and more than two instances of plagiarism, even at the high school level, should result in failure of the course. Two years of national service should be required, whether that service is military, educational, or social service (so that young people at eighteen must serve the United States through the armed forces, through working in public schools, or through working in social service agencies). There could be no deferments other than those for extreme disability. Rich or poor, married or unmarried, with children or without, all young people would serve—and then receive a free college education. This kind of national service can help to create connections, to see one's own privileges and the true suffering of others, and to help young people recognize that their needs and wants do not come first. So much of how young people understand themselves today—that they are the most important being in the whole world—gets reflected in plagiarism and other criminal activity. By providing hope for a better future, by providing a level playing field, by eliminating privilege at least for a little while, perhaps we can encourage teenagers to think beyond themselves and their often ridiculously silly worries so that they can see issues and ideas beyond their backyards.

Education

That leads to another kind of change needed. Education is of course an integral part of American culture, and it is working, almost intentionally, at promoting a pseudoscientific picture—at the expense of actual learning—of the children it purports to educate. Instead of holding children to specific standards of learning, to actual rigor, to facts, our educational system works from a set of philosophical and moral stances in an almost unconscious way. As demonstrated in chapter 5, our culture structures our educational system so that children's psychological "development" is privileged (at least, that of European American, middle-class children) over actually learning anything.

Schools seem far less interested in imparting knowledge than in promoting character education and children's self-esteem. As I have argued throughout this book, the focus on individualism in our culture is a profoundly immoral and unjust one. Our teachers have bought the entire picture, though, and they insist they actually know something about children. This is unfortunate in part because teachers ought to know something about a subject they are teaching, and, given the relatively low quality of students entering teaching lately, that kind of expertise seems unlikely.

In addition, though, the education profession seems to have swallowed, hook, line, and sinker the entire notion that children are unique and special, and that they have individual learning styles, and that their psyches are fragile and in need of constant boosting. Certainly the current idea is that children cannot fail without significant and negative emotional consequences, something that apparently must be avoided at all costs. The ability to think critically about developmental psychology seems lacking in education just as it is in psychology and many of the disciplines associated with the helping professions. What all of this means, though, is that education has been psychologized along with so many other parts of American culture, and that hyperindividualized psychologization is reflected in educational policy.

Even with the No Child Left Behind Act (which is leaving significant numbers of children behind, by the way), an apparent attempt to provide some kind of standardized curriculum and a common set of ideas that all children ought to be able to master, we see a failing educational system. In part, again, it seems to be because of the substandard quality of many teachers today—some analysts would argue that feminism has harmed the American educational system almost irreparably. Because of feminism, it is argued by some, the many talented women who became teachers some decades back did so because it, along with nursing and social work, was the only profession to which a "decent" woman could aspire. Now, however, highly intelligent and intellectually demanding women aim for more money and more prestige, leaving less talented women (and men) to fill the gaps as teachers in the K-12 system.

In addition, though, the educational system, like all other institutions in our society, is subject to fads and trends. The latest is the pseudoscientific description of children by child development experts, including "learning styles" and "diversity" and whole language instruction. This is all part of a larger post-modern moment in American culture, in which there is no surety, no authority, no challenge. Who is to say what constitutes a fact? This philosophical stance, permeating colleges of education, has led to a woefully undereducated populace. Perhaps those of us who are "content specialists" ought to be determining the subject matter of both colleges of education and the public school systems, since the educational "experts" don't seem to be doing any kind of job in teaching children today.

I would argue that there is a corpus of knowledge that all American children who graduate from high school ought to have in common: accurate science (including evolution), math through trigonometry, geography and map-reading abilities, basic writing abilities (accurate spelling, appropriate punctuation and capitalization, sentence and paragraph construction), basic reading abilities, a foundation in U.S. and world history, and some art and music appreciation. High school students, however, are graduating with few if any of these abilities. If our schools were funded adequately regardless of location, if poverty was eliminated, if teenagers were held to some specific behavioral and educational standards, perhaps we could catch up to the rest of the world educationally. As things stand now, however, we are in poor shape and we will only be falling further behind with the current educational ethos.

Families

American family life promotes incompetence and self-absorption as well. We seem to think a number of very odd things about family life. We think that the nuclear family is the "natural" family form, not recognizing its very real fragility in its emotional intensity. We think that it's appropriate to provide children with separate bedrooms and bathrooms, personal computers, individual televisions, adult sized beds and adult privileges and adult clothing—without demanding adult obligations from our children. Families, and, to a great extent, American life, lately seems to be so completely child-focused that it is a wonder any children are born. Parents seem to believe that anything a child wants trumps everything a parent wants. We have to wonder how parents ever have sex. Perhaps that explains the large number of one-child families in the United States. Certainly some parents believe that they cannot adequately raise more than one child, apparently thinking that a child must have undivided attention.

Well, piffle. Giving a child the full force attention of an adult seems to be leading to the narcissistic, self-absorbed, demanding children discussed throughout the book. And children who behave even worse than "normal" children who are, seemingly, merely "expressing" themselves, are not punished but therapized and, more frighteningly, drugged. Comedian Stephen Colbert, in his Comedy central television program *The Colbert Report* called this the phenomenon of "psychopharmoparenting" in one evening's "The Word" segment of the program (Colbert 2006). While humorous, Colbert's point is well taken: what used to be understood as normal childish behavior, requiring a parental punitive response, is now behavior that is a medical problem requiring a pharmaceutical solution. Parents no longer parent; they dispense drugs.

The only folks profiting from this state of affairs are the drug companies; children certainly are not terribly happy. Instead of human beings limiting the behavior of children—for example, parents and other adults taking charge—medications allegedly prevent the troublesome behavior to begin with. But one has to wonder how much creativity is being lost, and what kinds of long-term effects drugging children as we do will have. We have to assume, of course, that there will be physical long-term effects of some of the most popular children's drugs (Ritalin, for instance, and some anti-depressants such as Wellbutrin). But in addition the "medicalization of everyday life" (as Thomas Szasz [2007] calls it) will have consequences for American life down the road.

We already seem to expect not to ever feel bad. Even we adults, who ought to know better, will take antibiotics for viral infections, knowing that this does no good. All this kind of thing does is to help bacteria become more and more resistant to antibiotics. Sooner or later all of the drugs we take will result in many infections that can't be cured and instead that will kill us. We can extrapolate from there and consider how our tendency to drug ourselves for everything might ultimately result in a wish—to be fulfilled through pharmaceuticals—never to be unhappy, or uncomfortable, or unwell for a few days. The use of drugs to treat everyday life is so quintessentially American as to be almost laughable. America, the land of dreams, where anything is possible, the place of optimism and all good things, can only be had when using major drugs in significant quantities. And this is how we are managing our less-troubled children.

Those children in actual, serious distress—in foster care, abused, and so forth—are by and large abandoned by this country. They too have to be managed, so that most children in foster care are on one psychopharmaceutical drug or another and psychotherapy, but they are in many ways irrelevant to Americans. Perhaps we might pity them, but generally speaking "those" children seem to have little to do with "us." This particular stance, this neglect of our most vulnerable citizens (and even noncitizens) is so completely unjust and so shockingly immoral that it is difficult to know what to say. Clearly the anti-abortionists, if they were truly sincere about their passion for children, would ensure that no children were in foster care, including encouraging gay marriage and full adoption; they would promote tax and income equity; they would make sure that educational systems were fully funded. But they don't, of course. Anti-abortion proponents are among the most hypocritical in this nation, crying over fetuses but forgetting the actual existing children suffering within the child welfare system. As with so many issues of public policy, child welfare is built on neglect and immorality.

Mental illness

As may be clear by now, the language of psychotherapy and hyperindividualism is one of deep immorality. By insisting that human suffering is pretty much individually created, and thus individually handled, so much of the human experience is denied. We are denied connections to each other; we are denied the ability to take responsibility for others; we are denied the chance to be interdependent. The American treatment of mental illness is an example par excellence of these denials. Though so little of mental illness (or human behavior, for that matter) is truly established as biologically based, we Americans insist with greater and greater fervor that, in fact, just about everything is biological. We have an almost impossible time seeing culture in anything we do, and attempts to point out the cultural basis of human behavior, and suffering, are met with cries of indignation: "I don't make anyone feel anything, and nobody makes me do anything" is the frequent response. We have nothing to do with anyone else, in this formulation.

What's clear, though, from a rigorous examination of the literature as well as from cross-cultural evidence is that mental illnesses are almost exclusively cultural concoctions, generated by the needs of sociocultural systems, not biology and genetics. The existence of a wide variety of culture-bound syndromes demonstrates this. Americans continue to insist, though, that it is not us who have culture-bound syndromes, and there is a continual demand for research purporting to demonstrate the physiological basis for all abnormal behavior. Whether we are discussing anorexia, bulimia, addictions of various kinds, depression—you name it, there is a "scientist" out there insisting that poor choices and bad behaviors are biological diseases that can have a biological "cure," and that culture has nothing to do with it.

Such formulations are stunning in their simplistic nature and their complete lack of justice. Our insistence, over and over and over again, that people suffering with abnormal behavior are completely on their own is mind-boggling in its cruelty. We all have something to do with everyone's suffering—perhaps not directly but through agreeing with dominant American culture that suffering is due to individual defect. And, indeed, some of us do have something directly to do with others' suffering—family members who see their schizophrenic sibling as biologically ill rather than systemically created are participating in their sibling's suffering as thoroughly as if they were sticking knives in that person. Doctors who encourage this worldview are complicit as well—and, of course, doctors need mental illness to stay in business.

The business of mental illness allows for no compassion, for no remission of suffering. American culture needs mental illness to survive. If we were to start to see our obligations in creating and allowing depression, in encouraging bipolar disorder, in needing schizophrenia, or anorexia, or ADHD, and if we started to alter our behaviors so that depressive, bipolar, schizophrenic, anorexic, or hyperactive actions were diminished, not rewarded, redirected, perhaps the amount and kind of suffering so many Americans undergo would be lessened. If we saw our connections with each other, if we reduced our reliance on the language of psychotherapy and hyperindividualism as we dealt with those behaving oddly, and instead insisted on the acknowledgment that we are all part of each other's behaviors, perhaps, then, finally, we might be able to see all Americans as equals, as potentially competent.

Bigotry

But of course that is hard for many Americans. Seeing mental illness as culturally created is hard enough; we seem to be absolutely blind when it comes to institutionalized bigotry and discrimination. European Americans deny racism while insisting there are actual biological entities called "races" despite the complete lack of scientific evidence for it. European Americans think that it is the ignorant trash who cause the problems while they ignore their complicity in a profoundly discriminatory system. European Americans refuse to understand that bigotry is not just instantiated in the white sheets of the KKK but in the lack of choice historically oppressed peoples have in this country. When European Americans deny the reality of institutionalized bigotry and discrimination and, instead, insist it is they who are the victims lately, all justice is thrown out the window. Insisting as well that bigotry and discrimination are best fought with education, with changing hearts and minds, is a perfect American solution to a cultural problem. Instead of changing the culture, of a large-scale solution to a large-scale problem, the cultural response is diversity training and ethnic studies programs. Even we anthropologists can be complicit in these hyperindividualistic solutions if we're not careful. Simply insisting on cultural relativism can perpetuate our highly bigoted culture, since naïve anthropologists (or, more likely, those who are not anthropologists and romanticize concepts they don't really understand) might argue that we do not have a right to change a culture.

I am here to say that, as an anthropologist of European American descent, it is my duty to change American culture. In part, yes, this will be through providing my college students with a point of view and clearly established data they are unlikely to have ever heard before. Part of my duty, though, is to promote alternate policy constellations that fight discrimination and bigotry such as I do here.

Conclusion

Finally, then, what is there left to say? Anthropologists are perhaps best suited to comment on American society since we have the knowledge of the world beyond us, informing our interpretations of human behavior. We can "denaturalize" American behavior, exploding the folk science and the folk theories propounded by supposed experts (who are no more self-reflective than any other American) and putting all of this into cross-cultural context. We can, as the classic saying goes, "make the strange familiar and the familiar strange," pointing out that Americans, and American behaviors, are as culturally determined as the Yanamamo, the !Kung, the Swiss, or the Na. We can point out the American-ness of what we do. We can and must constantly comment on the language of psychotherapy and the insistence on hyperindividualism.

I believe that the first step is to recognize the moral vacuity of the psychotherapeutic metaphor.

The second stop is to stop invoking it all the time. Certainly there are circumstances when it is appropriate to discuss one's feelings. However, we need to find alternate metaphors, different languages to use to discuss, describe, and analyze behavior. We need to redefine the current American understanding of morality; we need to expand the concept, to allow for the judgment of public behavior and to let up, just a bit, on the judgment of private behavior. Our government—which is meant to be about all of us—needs to stop interfering in our bedrooms and needs to start interfering in our boardrooms. More harm has been done by the perpetrators of corporate financial scandals than any two gay men wanting to have a public demonstration of their commitment to one another (as the bumper sticker says: "Against gay marriage? Don't marry a gay person."). Our society has been positively hurt by unfettered corporate behaviors far more than it has by allowing women the right to control their fertility. Our continual invocation of the psychotherapeutic metaphor makes for overly dramatic, practically hysterical discussions of issues that are truly private in nature. Those same emotions seem absent from discussions of corporate malfeasance. Something is wrong with our society when we can point that out.

Finally, then, as a society, recognizing that the psychotherapeutic metaphor really has hurt our culture, harmed this country means that we need to affirm the connections we have with each other, both within our society and outside of it. We need to understand that we as individuals are not the center of the universe; we need to understand that we as a country have no right to impose our peculiar sets of understandings on other societies; we need to understand that we live in a global economy and a global ecology. We have responsibilities toward each other. Yes, we have rights we can claim.

But we have obligations as well, and it is time we began living up to them.

References

Abcfamily 2008. Gilmore Girls Page. http://abcfamily.go.com/abcfamily/path/section_Shows+GilmoreGirls/page_Detail (accessed August 14, 2008).

AFP. 2007. US War Contracts Top 25 Billion Dollars: Study. AFP, November 17, 2007. http://afp.google.com/article/ALeqM5gc8zVyl2UyurwxaWdnXg3XVug 7HA (accessed August 14, 2008).

Apuzzo, Matt. 2007. Gunman Left Note Raging against Women and Rich Kids. *Seattle Times*, April 17, 2007. http://seattletimes.nwsource.com/html/Nationworld/2003669403_shoot17.html (accessed February 7, 2008).

Associated Press. 2007. College Students Think They're *So* Special: Study Finds Alarming Rise in Narcissism, Self-centeredness in "Generation Me." MSNBC, February 27, 2007.

Auletta, Ken. 1982. *The Underclass*. New York: Random House.

Baker, Amy J.L. 2007. *Adult Children of Parental Alienation Syndrome: Breaking the Ties That Bind*. New York: W.W. Norton.

Belkin, Lisa. 2007. Life's Work: Parents Who Can't Resist Smoothing Life's Bumps. *New York Times*, February 11, 2007. http://www.nytimes.com/2007/02/11/business/yourmoney/11wcol.html?_r=1&scp=2&sq=Belkin%2C+Lisa&st=nyt&oref=slogin (accessed August 18, 2008).

Bellah, Robert, Richard Madsen, William M. Sullivan, Ann Swidler, and Steven M. Tipton. 1985. *Habits of the Heart: Individualism and Commitment in American Life*. New York: Harper and Row.

———. 1988. *Individual and Commitment in American Life: Readings on the Themes of Habits of the Heart*. New York: Harper and Row.

———. 1992. *The Good Society*. New York: Vintage.

Block, Melissa. 2007. Extremely Premature Baby Readies to Go Home. National Public Radio, *All Things Considered*, February 20, 2007. http://www.npr.org/templates/story/story.php?storyId=7500743 (accessed August 18, 2008).

Bly, Robert. 1996. *The Sibling Society*. New York: Vintage Books.

Bohlen, Anne, Kevin Rafferty, and James Ridgeway. 1991. *Blood in the Face*. Documentary film. http://www.imdb.com/title/tt0101479/ (accessed August 18, 2008).

Bordo, Susan. 1993. *Unbearable Weight: Feminism, Western Culture, and the Body*. Berkeley: University of California Press.

Brues, Alice M. 1997. Teaching about Race. In Conrad Kottak, Jane White, and Patricia White, eds., *The Teaching of Anthropology: Problems, Issues, and Decisions*, pp. 189–192. Mountain View, CA: Mayfield.

Brumberg, Joan Jacobs. 1997. The Appetite as Voice. In Carole Counihan and Penny Van Esterik, eds., *Food and Culture: A Reader*, pp. 159–179. New York: Routledge.

Bynum, Caroline Walker. 1997. Fast, Feast, and Flesh: The Religious Significance of Food to Medieval Women. In Carole Counihan and Penny Van Esterik, eds. *Food and Culture: A Reader*, pp. 138–158. New York: Routledge.

Campos, Paul. 2004. *The Obesity Myth: Why America's Obsession with Weight Is Hazardous to Your Health.* New York: Gotham.

Cann, R., M. Stoneking, and A. Wilson. 1987. Mitochondrial DNA and Human Evolution. *Nature* 325: 31–36.

Castillo, Richard J. 1997. *Culture and Mental Illness: A Client-Centered Approach.* Belmont, CA: Wadsworth.

Centers for Disease Control. 2005. Mental Health in the United States: Prevalence of Diagnosis and Medication Treatment for Attention-Deficit/Hyperactivity Disorder—United States, 2003. http://www.cdc.gov/mmwr/preview/mmwrhtml/mm5434a2.htm (accessed February 12, 2008).

Child Welfare League of America. n.d. The President's FY 2008 Budget and Children. http://www.cwla.org/advocacy/budgetchildren08.htm#tanf (accessed August 15, 2008).

Chriss, James J. 1999. *Counseling and the Therapeutic State.* New York: Aldine Transactional.

Clevand Clinic. 2004. http://www.clevelandclinicmeded.com/disease man agement/psychiatry/eating/table1.htm (accessed August 15, 2008).

Colbert, Stephen. 2006. *The Colbert Report: The Word.* July 11, 2006. http://www.tv.com/the-colbert-report/tony-hawk/episode/812982/sum mary.html (accessed August 15, 2008).

Consumer Product Safety Commission. 1999. CPSC Warns against Placing Babies in Adult Beds; Study Finds 64 Deaths Each Year from Suffocation and Strangulation. http://www.cpsc.gov/CPSCPUB/PREREL/PRHTML99/99175.html (accessed February 12, 2008).

Coontz, Stephanie. 1992.*The Way We Never Were: American Families and the Nostalgia Trap.* New York: Basic Books.

Davis, Merlene. 2008. Give Birth at Home? Why Not? *Lexington Herald-Leader*, February 12, 2008, pp. D1, D2.

Diamond, Jared. 1992. *The Third Chimpanzee: The Evolution and Future of the Human Animal.* New York: Harper Perennial.

———. 1999 *Guns, Germs, and Steel: The Fates of Human Societies.* New York: W.W. Norton.

Downey, Charles. 2000. That kid's really a character. *St. Louis Post-Dispatch*, Sept. 5, 2000, pp. E1, E3.

The Economist. 2007. After the Virginia Tech Massacre: America's Tragedy. April 19, 2007. http://www.economist.com/opinion/display story.cfm?story_id=9040170 (accessed February 7, 2008)

Ehrenreich, Barbara. 1990. *Fear of Falling: The Inner Life of the Middle Class*. New York: Harper Perennial.
———. 1997. The End of Caring. Alternative Radio. April 4, 1997, Portland, OR. Radio address transcript.
Epstein, William M. 1995. *The Illusion of Psychotherapy*. New Brunswick, NJ: Transaction.
———. 1997. *Welfare in America: How Social Science Fails the Poor*. Madison: University of Wisconsin.
———. 2002. *American Policy Making: Welfare as Ritual*. Lanham, MD: Rowman & Littlefield.
———. 2006. *Psychotherapy as Religion: The Civil Divine in America*. Reno: University of Nevada Press.
Eyer, Diane E. 1992. *Mother-Infant Bonding: A Scientific Fiction*. New Haven, CT: Yale University Press.
Fabrega, Horacio. 1982. Culture and Psychiatric Illness: Biomedical and Ethnomedical Concepts. In Geoffrey M. White and Anthony J. Marsella, eds., *Cultural Conceptions of Mental Health and Therapy*, pp. 39–68. Boston, MA: Reidel.
———. 2002. *Origins of Psychopathology: The Phylogenetic and Cultural Basis of Mental Illness*. New Brunswick, NJ: Rutgers University Press.
Fagan, Brian. 2004. *The Long Summer: How Climate Changed Civilization*. New York: Basic Books.
Feder, Kenneth L. 2003. *The Past in Perspective: An Introduction to Human Prehistory*. Boston, MA: McGraw Hill.
Fischer, Claude S., Michael Hout, Martín Sánchez Jankowski, Samuel R. Lucas, Ann Swidler, and Kim Voss. 1996. *Inequality by Design: Cracking the Bell Curve Myth*. Princeton, NJ: Princeton University Press.
Franck, Matthew. 2003. Missourians Caring for Grandchildren Face Cuts in Aid. *St. Louis Post-Dispatch*, July 13, 2003, pp. C1, C6.
Friedan, Betty. 1974. *The Feminine Mystique*. New York: Norton (Originally published 1963).
Gaines, Attwood. 1982. Cultural Definitions, Behavior, and the Person in American Psychiatry. In Geoffrey M. White and Anthony J. Marsella, *Cultural Conceptions of Mental Health and Therapy*, pp. 167–192. Boston, MA: Reidel.
Gard, Maisie C.E. and Chris P. Freeman. 1996.The Dismantling of a Myth: A Review of Eating Disorders and Socioeconomic Status. I*nternational Journal of Eating Disorders* 20: 1–12.
Geertz, Clifford. 1975. On the Nature of Anthropological Understanding. *American Scientist* 63: 47–53.
Gill, Dee and Eli Sanders. 2004. Minding Their Manners: A New Breed of Etiquette Classes for the Generation of Kids Raised on Bart Simpson and Britney Spears. *Time*, June 7, 2004, p. 55.
Gitlin, Todd. 1995. *The Twilight of Common Dreams: Why America Is Wracked by Culture Wars*. New York: Henry Holt, Owl Books.

Gordon, Linda. 1992. Social Insurance and Public Assistance: The Influence of Gender in Welfare Thought in the United States, 1890–1935. *American Historical Review* 97: 19–54.

———. 1994. Pitied But Not Entitled: Single Mothers and the Origin of Welfare. New York: Free Press.

Gremillion, Helen. 2003. *Feeding Anorexia: Gender and Power at a Treatment Center.* Durham, NC: Duke University Press.

Guisinger, Shan. 2003. Adapted to Flee Famine: Adding an Evolutionary Perspective on Anorexia Nervosa. *Psychological Bulletin* 110: 745–761.

Hafner, Katie. 2001. Lessons in Internet Plagiarism. *New York Times*, June 28, 2001. http://www.nytimes.com/2001/06/28/technology/28CHEA.html?ex=1210824000&en=40e7d6f9f54d0372&ei=5070 (accessed August 15, 2008).

Haley, Jay. 1982. *Leaving Home: The Therapy of Disturbed Young People.* New York: McGraw-Hill.

Hauser, Christine. 2007. Virginia Gunman Identified as Student. *New York Times*, April 17, 2007. http://www.nytimes.com/2007/04/17/us/17virginia.html?pagewanted=print (accessed February 7, 2008).

Heilbroner, Robert L. 1980. *The Making of Economic Society: Revised for the 1980s.* Englewood Cliffs, NJ: Prentice-Hall.

Heneghan, Kathleen. 2001. Court Case Questions Extended Breastfeeding (from *Mothering*, March 1, 2001) The Free Library (March 1, 2001), http://www.thefreelibrary.com/Court+Case+Questions+Extended+Breastfeeding-a076587460 (accessed February 5, 2008).

Hernnstein, Richard J. and Charles Murray. 1994. *The Bell Curve: Intelligence and Class Structure in American Life.* New York: Free Press.

Hrdy, Sarah Blaffer. 1999. *Mother Nature: Maternal Instincts and How They Shape the Human Species.* New York: Ballantine Books.

Jansson, Bruce S. 2001. *The Sixteen-Trillion Dollar Mistake: How the US Bungled Its National Priorities from the New Deal to the Present.* New York: Columbia University Press.

Kahn, Kim. n.d. The Basics: How Does Your Debt Compare? *MSN Money.* http://moneycentral.msn.com/content/SavingandDebt/P70581.asp (accessed February 8, 2008).

Kaminer, Wendy 1993. *I'm Dysfunctional, You're Dysfunctional: The Recovery Movement and Other Self-Help Fashions.* New York: Vintage Books.

Kasper, Rob. 2007. What a Mix: Gin, Tonic. *Baltimore Sun*, July 17, 2007. http://www.baltimoresun.com/entertainment/dining/bal-fo.beverage18jul17,0,4906307.story (accessed August 15, 2008).

Kasson, John F. 1990. *Rudeness & Civility: Manners in Nineteenth-Century Urban America.* New York: Hill and Wang.

Katz, Michael B. 1989. *The Undeserving Poor: From the War on Poverty to the War on Welfare.* New York: Pantheon Books.

———. 1996. *In the Shadow of the Poorhouse: A Social History of Welfare in America*. 10th anniversary edition. New York: Basic Books.

Kaufman, Leslie. 2006. A Dream Not Denied: Just a Normal Girl. *New York Times*, November 6, 2006. http://www.nytimes.com/2006/11/05/education/edlife/downs.html?ref=education (accessed August 15, 2008).

Keel, Pamela K. and Kathy L. Klump. 2003. Are Eating Disorders Culture-Bound Syndromes? Implications for Conceptualizing Their Etiology. *Psychological Bulletin* 129: 747–769.

Kirn, Walter 2002. I'm O.k. You're O.k. We're Not O.k. *Time*, September 16, 2002, p. 92.

Kleinman, Arthur and Byron Good, eds. 1985. *Culture and Depression: Studies in the Anthropology and Cross-Cultural Psychiatry of Affect and Disorder*. Berkeley: University of California Press.

Kluger, Jeffrey. 2003. Medicating young minds. *Time*, November 3, 2003, pp. 48–58.

Kluger, Jeffrey and Sora Song. 2002. Young and Bipolar. *Time*, August 19, 2002, pp. 40–51.

Kohn, Alfie. 2003. How Not to Teach Values. In James Wm. Noll, ed., *Taking Sides: Clashing Views on Controversial Educational Issues*, 12th edition, pp. 102–117. Guilford, CT: McGraw-Hill/Dushkin.

Kottak, Conrad Phillip. 2008. *Cultural Anthropology*. 12th edition. Boston, MA: McGraw Hill.

Krugman, Paul. 2007. *The Conscience of a Liberal*. New York: W.W. Norton.

KSDK-TV. 2003. Story on Cruising in Fairgrounds Park (St. Louis). *News at Noon*, June 25, 2003.

Kuper, Adam. 1996. *The Chosen Primate: Human Nature and Cultural Diversity*. Cambridge, MA: Harvard University Press.

Kurtz, Stanley N. 1992. *All the Mothers Are One: Hindu India and the Cultural Reshaping of Psychoanalysis*. New York: Columbia University Press.

Kusserow, Adrie. 2004. *American Individualisms: Child Rearing and Social Class in Three Neighborhoods*. New York: Palgrave Macmillan.

Kutchins, Herb and Stuart A. Kirk. 1997. *Making Us Crazy: DSM: The Psychiatric Bible and the Creation of Mental Disorders*. New York: Free Press.

Laurance, Jeremy. 2008. Anti-Depressant Drugs Don't Work—Official Study. *The Independent* (England), February 26, 2008. http://www.independent.co.uk/life-style/health-and-wellbeing/health-news/antidepressant-drugs-udontu-work-ndash-official-study-787264.html (accessed August 15, 2008).

Lebra, Takie S. 1982. Self-reconstruction in Japanese Religious Psychotherapy. In Geoffrey M. White and Anthony J. Marsella, *Cultural Conceptions of Mental Health and Therapy*, pp. 269–284. Boston, MA: Reidel.

Lee, Christopher. 2007. Bush: No Deal on Children's Health Plan. President Says He Objects on Philosophical Grounds. *Washington Post*, July 19, 2007, p. A03 (online).

Lester, Rebecca. 1995. Embodied Voices: Women's Food Asceticism and the Negotiation of Identity. *Ethos* 23: 187–222.

Lewin, Tamar. 2001. Class Time and Not Jail Time for Anger, But Does It Work? *New York Times*, July 1, 2001. Through Lexis-Nexis.

Lewis, Oscar. 1959. *Five Families: Mexican Case Studies in the Culture of Poverty*. New York: Basic Books.

———. 1963. *The Children of Sanchez: Autobiography of a Mexican Family*. New York: Vintage Books.

———. 1965. *La Vida: A Puerto Rican Family in the Culture of Poverty—San Juan and New York*. New York: Random House.

Lieberman, Leonard and Rodney Kirk. 1997. Teaching about Human Variation: An Anthropological Tradition for the Twenty-First Century. In Conrad Kottak, Jane White, and Patricia White, eds., *The Teaching of Anthropology: Problems, Issues, and Decisions*, pp. 193–207. Mountain View, CA: Mayfield.

Linn, Susan. 2005. *Consuming Kids: Protecting Our Children from the Onslaught of Marketing & Advertising*. New York: Anchor Books.

Lock, Margaret. 1982. Popular Conceptions of Mental Health in Japan. In Geoffrey M. White and Anthony J. Marsella, eds., *Cultural Conceptions of Mental Health and Therapy*, pp. 215–234. Boston, MA: Reidel.

Lutz, Catherine. 1985. Depression and the Translation of Emotional Worlds. In Arthur Kleinman and Byron Good, eds., *Culture and Depression: Studies in the Anthropology and Cross-cultural Psychiatry of Affect and Disorder*, pp. 63–100. Berkeley: University of California Press.

Marks, Jonathan. 2003. *What It Means to Be 98% Chimpanzee: Apes, People, and Their Genes*. Berkeley: University of California Press.

McElvaine, Robert. 2001. *Eve's Seed: Biology, the Sexes, and the Course of History*. New York: McGraw-Hill.

McIntosh, Peggy. 1988. White Privilege: Unpacking the Invisible Knapsack. http://www.case.edu/president/aaction/UnpackingTheKnapsack.pdf (accessed August 15, 2008).

Minuchin, Salvador. 1974. *Families and Family Therapy*. Cambridge, MA: Harvard University Press.

———. 1981. *Family Therapy Techniques*. Cambridge, MA: Harvard University Press.

Moynihan, Daniel Patrick. 1965. The Negro Family: The Case for National Action. http://www.dol.gov/oasam/programs/history/webid-meynihan.htm (accessed August 15, 2008).

MSNBC. 2008. Shooter's Rampage Baffles Friends. MSNBC, February 16, 2008. http://www.msnbc.msn.com/id/23171567/ (accessed March 11, 2008).

Murphy, Mary Beth. 1998a. Cleveland a Pioneer in Neighborhood Foster Care. *Milwaukee Journal Sentinel*, June 7, 1998, pp. 1A, 12A.

Murphy, J.M. 1976. Psychiatric Labeling in Cross-Cultural Perspective. *Science*, March 12, 1976, pp. 1019–1028

———. 1998b. Cleveland's Foster Care System Encourages Families to Be Partners. *Milwaukee Journal Sentinel*, June 8, 1998, pp. 1A, 7A.

National Endowment for the Arts. 2007. *To Read or Not to Read: A Question of National Consequence.* Washington, DC: National Endowment for the Arts.

National Institute of Mental Health. 2004. http://www.nimh.nih.gov/pub licat/eatingdisorders.cfm (accessed February 8, 2008).

———. 2008. The Numbers Count: Mental Illness in America. February 7, 2008. http://www.nimh.nih.gov/health/publications/the-numbers-count-mental-disorders-in-america.shtml#Schizophrenia (accessed February 8, 2008).

New York Times. 2008. H.I.V. Rises among Young Gay Men. *New York Times*, January 14, 2008. http://www.nytimes.com/2008/01/14/opinion/14mon2.html (accessed February 12, 2008).

Newman, Abby Margolis n.d. Raising a Reader: Teachers Build Skills, But a Parent's Top Job Is to Nurture a Love of Books and Words. *Scholastic Parents*. http://content.scholastic.com /browse/article.jsp?id=1522 (accessed February 7, 2008).

Newport, Frank. 2007. Just Why Do Americans Attend Church? Gallup.com: http://www.gallup.com/poll /27124/Just-Why-Americans-Attend-Church.aspx#1 (accessed February 5, 2008)

Oppenheimer, Stephen. 2003. *The Real Eve: Modern Man's Journey Out of Africa*. New York: Carroll & Graf.

Park, Alice. 2004. The Psychological Reasons: What Deep Inner Urges Drive Some People to Overeat and Others to Starve Themselves? *Time*, June 7, 2004, p. 76.

Passel, Jeffrey S., Randolph Capps, and Michael E. Fix. 2004. Undocumented Immigrants: Facts and Figures. The Urban Institute, January 12, 2004. http://www.urban.org/Publications/1000587.html (accessed August 15, 2008).

Peshkin, Alan. 1994. *Growing Up American: Schooling and the Survival of Community*. Prospect Heights, IL: Waveland Press.

Pitts, Leonard. 2008. Living with Injustice. *Miami Herald*, May 14, 2008. http://www.miamiherald.com/living/columnists/leonard_pitts/story/532336.html (accessed August 15, 2008).

Postman, Neil. 1994. *The Disappearance of Childhood*. New York: Vintage Books.

Putnam, Robert D. 2000. *Bowling Alone: The Collapse and Revival of American Community*. New York: Simon & Schuster.

Quart, Alissa. 2003. *Branded: The Buying and Selling of Teenagers*. Cambridge, MA: Perseus.

Ravitch, Diane. 2003. *The Language Police: How Pressure Groups Restrict What Students Learn*. New York: Alfred A. Knopf.

Reich, Walter. 2000. Can Psychology Cure Racism? *Slate*, January 13, 2000. http://www.slate.com/id/72826/entry/72878/ (accessed August 15, 2008).

Rector, Robert E. 2007. How Poor Are America's Poor? Examining the "Plague" of Poverty in America. The Heritage Foundation, August 27, 2007. http://www.heritage.org/Research/Welfare/bg2064.cfm (accessed August 15, 2008).

Reid, Robert, George J. DuPaul, Thomas J. Powers, Arthur D. Anastopoulos, Diana Rogers-Adkinson, Mary-Beth Noll, and Cynthia Riccio. 1998. Assessing Culturally Different Students for Attention Deficit Hyperactivity Disorder Using Behavior Rating Scales. *Journal of Abnormal Child Psychology* 28: 187–198.

Ritter, Malcolm. 2007. Teen Brains Likened to Cars with Weak Brakes. *Lexington* (KY) *Herald-Leader*, December 17, 2007, pp. A1, A10.

Roach, John. 2006. Young Americans Geographically Illiterate, Survey Suggests. *National Geographic News*, May 2, 2006. http://news.nationalgeographic.com/ news/2006/05/0502_060502_geography.html (accessed February 12, 2008).

Roberts, Michael. 2005. The Origins of Modern Humans: Multiregional and Replacement Theories. http://calvin.linfield.edu/~mrobert/origins.htm (accessed August 15, 2008).

Rocca, Francis X. 2007. Pope Says Abortion, Gay Marriage Are "Obstacles" to World Peace. Pew Forum on Religion and Public Life, December 17, 2007 http://pewforum.org/news/display.php?NewsID=14597 (accessed February 12, 2008).

Rogers, Susan Carol. 1975. Female Forms of Power and the Myth of Male Dominance: A Model of Female/Male Interaction in Peasant Society. *American Ethnologist* 2: 727–756.

Roland, Alan. 1988. *In Search of Self in India and Japan: Toward a Cross-Cultural Psychology*. Princeton: Princeton University Press.

Ryan, William. 1976. *Blaming the Victim*. New York: Vintage.

Scheper-Hughes, Nancy. 1993. *Death Without Weeping: The Violence of Everyday Life in Brazil*. Berkeley, CA: University of California Press.

Schneider, Jo Anne. 1999. And How Are We Supposed to Pay for Health Care? Views of the Poor and the Near Poor on Welfare Reform. *American Anthropologist* 101: 761–782.

Scott, Eugenie C. 2004. *Evolution vs. Creationism: An Introduction*. Berkeley: University of California Pres.

Secombe, Karen. 1999. *"So You Think I Drive a Cadillac?": Welfare Recipients' Perspectives on the System and Its Reform*. Boston, MA: Allyn & Bacon.

Shipler, David K. 2004. *The Working Poor: Invisible in America*. New York: Alfred A. Knopf.

Shreeve, James. 1995. *The Neanderthal Enigma: Solving the Mystery of Modern Origins*. New York: Avon Books.

Shweder, Richard A. and Edmund J. Bourne. 1991. Does the Concept of the Person Vary Cross-culturally? In Richard A. Shweder, ed., *Thinking through Cultures: Expeditions in Cultural Psychology*, pp. 113–155. Cambridge, MA: Harvard University Press.

Simons, Ronald C. and Charles C. Hughes, eds. 1985. *The Culture-Bound Syndromes: Folk Illness of Psychiatric and Anthropological Interest.* Dordrecht, Holland: D. Reidel.

Small, Meredith. 1998. *Our Babies, Ourselves: How Biology and Culture Shape the Way We Parent.* New York: Anchor Books.

———. 2006. *The Culture of Our Discontent: Beyond the Medical Model of Mental Illness.* Washington, DC: Joseph Henry Press.

Specht, Harry and Mark Courtney. 1994. *Unfaithful Angels: How Social Work Has Abandoned Its Mission.* New York: Free Press.

Stacy, Judith. 1996. *In the Name of the Family: Rethinking Family Values in the Postmodern Age.* Boston, MA: Beacon Press.

Suppes, Mary Ann and Carolyn Cressy Wells. 2003. *The Social Work Experience: An Introduction to Social Work and Social Welfare.* Boston, MA: McGraw-Hill.

Sykes, Charles J. 1995. Losing the Education Race. http://www.sntp.net/education/education_stats.htm (accessed February 7, 2008).

Szasz, Thomas. 2007. *The Medicalization of Everyday Life: Selected Essays.* Syracuse, NY: Syracuse University Press.

Tattersall, Ian. 2002. *The Monkey in the Mirror: Essays on the Science of What Makes Us Human.* San Diego: Harvest Harcourt.

Thompson, Becky. 1994. Food, Bodies, and Growing Up Female: Childhood Lessons about Culture, Race, and Class. In Patricia Fallon, Melanie A. Katzman, and Susan C. Wooley, eds., *Feminist Perspectives on Eating Disorders*, pp. 355–378. New York: Guilford.

Throop, Elizabeth. 1991. Bounded and Embedded: Concepts and Experience of the Self Cross-culturally. Unpublished manuscript.

———. 1992. You're Driving Me Crazy: Family Dynamics and Schizophrenia in the West and India. Unpublished Master's thesis.

———. 1995. Authority, Hierarchy, and Education: Childrearing Patterns and Irish and Hindu College Students. Paper delivered to Wheaton (IL) College Department of Sociology and Anthropology Colloquium, November 11, 1997.

———. 1999. *Net Curtains and Closed Doors: Intimacy, Family, and Public Life in Dublin.* Westport, CT: Bergin & Garvey.

Tice, Carol. 2003. Casey Foundation to Offer $1M in Anti-poverty Grants. *Puget Sound Business Journal*, August 1, 2003. http://seattle.bizjournals.com/seattle/stories/2003/08/04/newscolumn3.html (accessed February 8, 2008).

U.S. Census Bureau. 2008. Historical Income Tables—Households. http://www.census.gov/hhes/www/income/histinc/h01ar.html (accessed August 15, 2008).

USA Today. 2007. Fla. Baby Delivered at 21 Weeks Won't Go Home as Planned. *USA Today*, February 20, 2007. http://www.usatoday.com/news/health/2007–02–20-tiny-baby_x.htm (accessed August 15, 2008).

Vitz, Paul C. 1977. *Psychology as Religion: The Cult of Self-Worship.* Grand Rapids, MI: William B. Eerdmans.

Way, Karen. 1995. Never Too Rich . . . or Too Thin: The Role of Stigma in the Social Construction of Anorexia Nervosa. In Donna Maurer, and Jeffery Sobal, eds., *Eating Agendas: Food and Nutrition as Social Problems*, pp. 91–113. New York: Aldine de Gruyter.

Welch, Liz. 2003. Grandparents to the Rescue. *Parade Magazine*, July 20, 2003, pp. 4–5.

White, Geoffrey M. and Anthony J. Marsella. 1982. Introduction: Cultural Conceptions in Mental Health Research and Practice. In Geoffrey M. White and Anthony J. Marsella, eds., *Cultural Conceptions of Mental Health and Therapy*, pp. 3–38. Boston, MA: Reidel.

White, Geoffrey M. 1982. The Ethnographic Study of Cultural Knowledge of "Mental Disorder." In Geoffrey M. White and Anthony J. Marsella, eds., *Cultural Conceptions of Mental Health and Therapy*, pp. 69–96. Boston, MA: Reidel.

Wikan, Unni. 1990. *Managing Turbulent Hearts: A Balinese Formula for Living.* Chicago: University of Chicago Press.

Wilgoren, Jodi. 2001. School Cheating Scandal Tests Town's Value. *New York Times*, February 4, 2002. http://query.nytimes.com/gst/fullpage.html?res=9F06E1DE143FF937A25751C0A9649C8B63&sec=&spon=&pagewanted=2 (accessed August 15, 2008).

Wolf, Naomi. 1994. Hunger. In Patricia Fallon, Melanie A. Katzman, and Susan C. Wooley, eds., *Feminist Perspectives on Eating Disorders*, pp. 94–111. New York: Guilford.

World Health Organization. n.d. Schizophrenia. http://www.who.int/mental_health/management/schizophrenia/en/ (accessed February 12, 2008). 2004. www.who.org.

Wormer, Katherine van. 1997. *Social Welfare: A World View.* Chicago: Nelson-Hall.

Yanagisako, Sylvia Junko. 1987. Mixed Metaphors: Native and Anthropological Models of Gender and Kinship Domains. In Jane Fishburne Collier and Sylvia Junko Yanagisako, eds., *Gender and Kinship: Essays toward a Unified Analysis*, pp.86–118. Stanford, CA: Stanford University Press.

Zielenziger, Michael. 2006. *Shutting Out the Sun: How Japan Created Its Own Lost Generation.* New York: Nan A. Talese/Doubleday.

Zuckerman, Laurence. 2000. Works in Progress from All Over; Discovering a Deficit in Attention Deficit. *New York Times*, January 1, 2000. http://query.nytimes.com /gst/fullpagehtml?res=9A0CE3DE1238F932A35752C0 A9669C8B63 (accessed February 7, 2008).

Index